# St. Columba's Seat and a Touch of Serendipity

## ... A short Story ...

## Peter Gatenby

GHP

**Grosvenor House
Publishing Limited**

This book is published by
Grosvenor House Publishing Ltd
Link House
140 The Broadway, Tolworth, Surrey, KT6 7HT.
www.grosvenorhousepublishing.co.uk

This book is a work of fiction. Any resemblance to
people or events, past or present, is purely coincidental.

A CIP record for this book
is available from the British Library

ISBN 978-1-83615-250-7

This story is dedicated to my beautiful wife Jill,
who I first met by a touch of serendipity nearly sixty years ago.

# Contents

| | | |
|---|---|---|
| | Prologue | vii |
| Chapter 1 | Tongue to Inverbroch | 1 |
| Chapter 2 | The Precocious Girl | 7 |
| Chapter 3 | The Tragedy | 13 |
| Chapter 4 | The Long Road to Solace | 21 |
| Chapter 5 | A Touch of Serendipity | 31 |
| Chapter 6 | The Ceilidh | 39 |
| Chapter 7 | We're Sitting in the Picture! | 47 |
| Chapter 8 | A Double Celebration | 59 |
| Chapter 9 | Compatibility Gets Checked! | 77 |
| Chapter 10 | Is it All Too Good to Be true? | 95 |
| Chapter 11 | The Workshop Takes Shape | 109 |
| Chapter 12 | The Wedding is Planned | 121 |
| Chapter 13 | Oh Yes, I Will | 139 |
| | Epilogue | 157 |
| | About the Author | 159 |

# Prologue

Now we are in the 21$^{st}$ century, most children born after the year 2000 have little appreciation of how the world was when their grandparents or great grandparents grew up.

Early in the 20$^{th}$ century most Scottish villages would have enough basic trades, so you would not have to go far to gather the basic needs of a family. A village grocer, a butcher, a post office, a church, and probably a pub. The population that was not employed in the aforementioned trades or shops might be crofters or farmers, or perhaps builders or carpenters. You may even have had a tailor or seamstress living nearby. The population was large enough for marriages to take place between families that could have known each other for generations.

However, after two world wars, this rather insulated village life where you rarely ventured to the large towns of say Stirling, Inverness, or perhaps Edinburgh, all changed. Indeed, as men returned to the small villages, they yearned for the "modern" aspirations now so evident in these larger towns. The subsistence living was no longer enough, and this led to a steady decline in village populations. A key indicator was the size of the congregation on Sunday at the local church. Indeed, the list of redundant churches up for sale is a sad reflection of how attitudes to daily life have changed.

Nevertheless, all is not lost; there are still a few determined souls who are trying to buck the trend, and enterprising community councils will not only do all they can to attract tourists, but also encourage local enterprises, even if it is just a pottery or an outdoor sports centre.

One such town is Inverbroch, which sadly has lost the use of its church, but has wisely joined with its larger neighbour a few miles away to spread the cost of services such as education and be able to better monitor planning applications. Thus, they can ensure these proposals are appropriate and not putting local services, such as water and sewerage, under too much pressure.

Inverbroch rests near the estuary of the river that flows down from a dam and a hydro-electric power station. At present it has a grocery store, a craft shop, a café, and a hotel, as well as a community hall. There are number of buildings which have been done up and are available as holiday lets, as well as several B&Bs, which provide enough employment opportunities for the local population. The community council are always looking for new enterprises that will fit in with existing trades and not create disturbance or besmirch the beautiful countryside all about. Thus, they are careful to manage the inevitable need for wind farms or hydraulic power stations.

One key attraction for the more active visitors to our village is the Great Glen Way — a long-distance path of 79 miles from Fort William to Inverness, which passes through and above our mystery town and many readers will already recognise. Indeed, the writer has traversed most of the Great Glen Way and stayed at a B&B at Inverbroch on his journeys to the *"four corners of the known world"*, as he would call them. These are his walks to the four extremities, being the furthest points East, West, South, and North of the British mainland.

So, now we had better start our story of how two quietly determined artistic and brave children of generation Z, as they seem to be called these days, brought life and joy to Inverbroch.

While they attended the same academy, they were in a different school year. But it was a timely act of serendipity that would bring them together and, like the north and south of two magnets once together, there was no pulling them apart.

# Chapter 1

# Tongue to Inverbroch

John Mackay, the father of our shy hero called James, lived at Tongue, where many of the Mackay clan had been for generations. It is only, however, in recent years that they have bestowed the nominal title to the land primarily occupied by Clan Mackay and in 2004 erected signs along the approaching roads saying **Mackay County**. The land is part of the Scottish county of Sutherland, which the reader may think is a strange name to give to a northerly county of Scotland. However, the most north-easterly part of what you may think should be Sutherland is Caithness-shire. Also, it is likely that the county of Sutherland got its name from the land owner Forby Sutherland.

James was born just before Christmas on Friday, 19th December, 2003. His father John and mother Katherine doted on their son who, as you would expect from a Friday child, was *loving and giving*. He quickly adapted to his surroundings and even at nursery school seemed to be more interested in how the limited daylight in the winter — at the time of his birth — gave strange shapes to the mountains about him. He was quick to know the difference between deciduous and coniferous trees and noted how you could tell the type of tree from the shape of its leaves as well as the angle the branches came off from the main trunk.

His father initially had many different jobs, but in July 2008 saw an advert to work for the Scottish Forestry. This would mean a move to the east side of Scotland. So, at the beginning of the autumn term on Monday, 18th August, our wee laddie found himself at a primary school just a short walk from the start of Loch Ness, in a town called Wadesburgh.

Initially, the family rented a small house, but after about nine months they had saved up a deposit, and with a stable employment history could get a mortgage to buy a property called Rubha Ard. This house was all but on the Great Glen Way, above the village of Inverbroch, which worked well. A school bus would pick up young James from the hotel car park below the house at 8:10am sharp and bring him back at about 16:15pm. Meanwhile, his father was often working in the forests nearby, along the shores of Loch Ness. And in the winter months John would often be home before his son, because the daylight hours were so short.

The village had a small, but sturdy snow plough, which could be attached to the front of Mr Mackay's Jeep. And when working away was not possible, John would be shifting snow from the minor roads in the village to allow people to get to the shops. The main road was, of course, the responsibility of Transport Scotland.

While at primary school, James excelled at art — or as it might better be described at his age, painting. He was forever doodling small sketches on the side of his workbooks of views out of the school windows, or even a sunrise over Loch Ness which he'd noted as the bus came down the main road to school.

He was a shy boy, but the lack of interaction with his peer group did not worry him. However, things changed a little when he went up to senior school.

While the teachers could not stop groups of girls and boys gathering to discuss their latest pop idol, or discuss how they would be supporting the local football team, they tried to ensure that discipline was maintained both in and out of school. "Bad behaviour will reflect back on the school, so use your surplus energies, to do something nice and helpful," the head teacher would often say at the morning assembly on Fridays.

"So, today I am adding Lawrence Cameron's name to the *Scroll of Honour* for his quick thinking in stopping the traffic when a young girl fell off her bike in a recent heavy shower of rain. This had reduced visibility, so a nasty fall could have become a tragic accident. It seems our Lawrence keeps in his pocket a flashing red light that would normally be attached to a bicycle. So, he started it flashing then quickly and carefully stepped out to stop the traffic. Our community police officer was most impressed by this act. Lawrence continued to assist the young girl, even ringing his father who drives a truck, asking him to come quickly into town so they could load the bicycle onto the back and take the girl — who I am glad to say was not badly hurt — home to her parents in Inverbroch.

"I want to see a lot more acts of kindness acknowledged by other names being added to the Roll before the end of term. However, remember being kind and thoughtful children is something you should be doing 365 days a year, not just in term time."

This attitude built into the school's ethos was something the parents were very happy to support. When you live in a relatively small community and almost everybody is known by somebody else, a community spirit is essential.

Each year the school held a Fete, and half the money raised would go to a charity the children chose to support that year, with the other half to the Matilda Fund. This fund had been set up with the schools blessing after one of their pupils, 12-year-old Matilda Hawkins, had dropped dead in the middle of a hockey match, having had an undetected heart defect.

The girl's parents were, of course, devastated by the death of their caring, helpful child. However, as a tribute to their daughter's caring attitude, they asked for the fund to be set up to provide money to support local residents who had fallen on hard times.

With a friendly, caring attitude impressed upon pupils, you would think that our James should have no concerns about moving to the senior school, which was on the same campus. Nevertheless, it is much more difficulty to corral belligerent children over the age of 11 and physically much stronger and sometimes as tall as their teachers. The friendship code instilled in them since starting school should mean they respected their teachers, as well as each other, and not deliberately cause a nuisance.

However, there tended to be what might be called groupings rather than gangs, and you were either in one of these groups or an outsider. The leader of one of these groups — Bruce Sparling — would shout derogatory comments whenever he saw James, thinking his followers would somehow think he was a brave and noble warrior. But most laughed out of a misguided impression that supporting the belligerent Bruce strengthened their own status. James ignored these comments, some of which were most hurtful, implying his mother was running a brothel.

"Probably she has a red light flashing in her window, like that Lawrence fellow," said Bruce, at which as his crew would cheer and think it was a great joke.

James's father had realised his son was a rather timid but respectful child so gave him some words of advice. "You will find you come across many problems as you grow up," he would often say. "Manage the problem and learn to find people you can trust. Every problem has a solution or can be circumvented."

Indeed, James did find a solution that worked well most days. The lunch break was one hour 15 minutes, but James only needed 15 minutes to eat his lunch then he would be off to chess club which was held at the end of the music room. Obviously, a loud brash Bruce would have been kicked out very quickly, especially as there were often extra music classes going on at the same time.

So, for the year 2014/15 James coped well enough, having just a couple of friends he would play chess with.

One thing that did happen of note was that one of the signs showing you were entering Mackay County was vandalised, and this got a lot of mention in the press, so much so that a bright lad in James's class called out, *"Here comes the County Man."*

James was the only Mackay in the school, as of course it was a surname primarily found in the northwest of Sutherland. Over the years, the nickname stuck. James did not mind particularly; indeed, he felt it more as a badge of honour, as none of his classmates could claim the accolade of having a county named after them.

As the years went past, James coped well enough, having just one true friend — his lunchtime chess partner, Lawrence Cameron. His reports showed he was attentive and made an effort even in subjects that were academic. He was never at the top of his class but still gained good marks. His art work, though, was exceptionally good, and he gained a reputation for being a shy Claude Monet.

*Chapter 2*

# The Precocious Girl

While our wee James was growing up as a timid but respectful young artist, there was a young girl who was always more grown up than her years would suggest. Emily Macdonald lived quite close to the school and had been born on 9th June, 2002, so was 18 months older than James. Perhaps importantly, she was a school year ahead of James, and ordinarily their paths would not cross. They might have unknowingly rubbed shoulders as they passed along the corridors of the school building on their way to classes, but they were never in the same classroom at the one time.

Even at the tender age of 12, Emily was what might be called a "head turner". She was a tall girl with leaf green eyes, high cheekbones, a natural smile, and she kept her black, slightly wavy hair just above shoulder length. However, Emily did not let her good looks go to her head. Indeed, she was a highly intelligent but determined soul who, from the tender age of ten, had already decided what she wanted to do. On a school visit to a pottery, she tried her hand — very successfully, one might add — at making a pot. She had a natural, steady hand and an eye for shape and form. She marvelled how a simple glaze poured over the soft clay and then heated in a kiln could change something that seemed rather fragile and not even waterproof into a useful item.

So, from a very early age Emily was developing her skills in art design, and often the teacher would say cheekily "How is our Charles Rennie Mackintosh today?"

Emily would take this in good heart, as she knew full well that Mackintosh was one of Scotland's leading architects. She actually felt a hereditary link with the "master", as he had married a Margaret Macdonald, which happened also to be the name of Emily's mother, so in theory they could be related.

In the early years, often just yards away but in another class, James sat concentrating on his Maths or English and continuing to excel at any subject that required a dextrous hand, such as technical drawing. The forward-looking school included the subject in the curriculum for any pupil who might have a natural ability in this field.

The years went by, and our two pupils both earned a name for their artistic merits.

Emily, being the assertive, intelligent, tall girl, was not only top of her class but was chosen as deputy head girl when only 16. She gained a large following of friends at school, even though a Prefect, and therefore had some limited powers over her fellow pupils. However, she developed the skill of quickly calming any rumpus that occurred.

Part of her ability to assert her authority over girls, as well as boys, came from the fact that she had an elder brother who was some four years older. So, Emily had quickly learned how to stem any family argument and keep the peace. Emily was also tall for her age and had this almost frighteningly penetrating stare, so when she approached even the most belligerent child, he or she simply stopped what they were doing. Often, Emily would come up and make some humorous or even confusing comment.

"Should I be wearing boxing gloves to join in, or can you lend me yours?" she might say.

This confounded both sides of the confrontation, who of course were not wearing boxing gloves but stopped what they were doing to understand what she meant. This allowed tempers to cool a little, offering Emily the chance to quietly discuss the cause of the upset, acting like Judge Judy as arbiter. In most cases, the parties separated, if not friends, at least not enemies.

Over the months it was noted how there was very little trouble, if any, while Emily was in the playground at breaktimes. There would of course be a duty teacher around, but in most cases they had little to do other than check with Emily that any unruly behaviour was suitably settled, and the matter did not need any official recording or further action.

One memorable occasion illustrates how Emily's unconventional approach could change a minor rumpus into something positive. Two boys that she knew and would normally be considered friends were shouting and nearly coming to blows when Emily approached them. Before she could even ask what the squabble was about, Rupert shouted, "He pinched my new pen!"

"Well, Donald, I think perhaps you have taken it, on a very temporary basis, and will now be handing it back?"

Then, giving both boys one of her famous frightening stares, she added, "I thought you two boys were friends."

This, of course, slightly embarrassed the boys, and they knew you did not want to upset the Deputy Head Girl. So, the pen was quickly returned and a brief sorry said by Donald.

Emily, looking around the playground, told them, "Well, now that you are friends again, I want you to pick up all the rubbish that is blowing around and place it in the bins by the bike shed. I am not sure where it has all come from, but I am sure you two will be able to show you are good citizens and have the place looking spick and span before the bell goes,

9

which gives you just 20 minutes. If it is the high standard of cleanliness that shows the school off in a good light, there may be a reward. So, step to it."

The boys, wondering what the reward might be, rushed off and soon had the playground looking very smart. Where possible they placed the cans and cardboard, as well as paper, in the correct recycling bins, and with two minutes to spare found Emily to see what the reward might be.

Emily produced a £5 note from her pocket. However, she hesitated before passing it over to the boys, who were thinking they were going to be rich.

Emily then asked Donald about his mother. "Did I hear she had to go into hospital?"

"Yes," said Donald, "but she is home now."

"Oh good," said Emily. "Now, no good turn goes unpunished, so you won't spend this money on sweets. Instead, you will call at the flower shop just at the top of town and buy a small posy of flowers for Donald's mum which both of you will present to her this evening. I am sure if you explain that you want to buy a small posy of flowers for your mother, Donald, Mrs Kelsey at the flower shop can oblige you. And no cheating. You will spend all the money on the flowers, understood?"

The boys both nodded and, slightly disappointed, took the £5 note.

Emily's mum, who knew Donald's mother, later heard the rest of the story. The boys did indeed get a rather nice but small posy and presented it to her, and she was naturally delighted and pleased with her kind and thoughtful son.

But then suddenly she said, "Where did you get the money to buy the flowers from?" She was concerned that it may have been stolen.

"We had to clean up the playground, because when the rubbish men came there was a huge wind and an awful lot of it blew around, landing at the north end by the sports hall."

"So, who gave you the money then?"

"The Deputy Head Girl Emily Macdonald. She gave us a £5 note, but then said, 'no good turn goes unpunished'!"

With that, Donald's mother burst out laughing. "That sounds like Emily, from what her mother has told me. Come on, you two, get the orange squash out of the fridge, and I'll see what I can find in my biscuit tin."

With the boys seated at the kitchen table, she produced some Jaffa Cakes which of course was the sort of prize the boys appreciated.

By the autumn of 2019, Emily had risen to be Head Girl, and in that term a young girl called Aileen Murphy entered the school. Her father had gained a prestigious, well-paid job in overall charge of the Hydro-Electric Power Stations in the area, so her family's move from Ireland was rather forced on her. She was a little younger than Emily but was slightly hampered by being thrust into the Scottish Education system just when she had worked out the subjects she wanted to study in Ireland. As a result, she had to rejig the subjects to fit in with the Scottish Credit Qualifications Framework. In her previous school she had been "top dog", being a senior Prefect.

However, while Emily had developed a humorous method of calming any confrontation with her almost wicked wit, Aileen had used a more aggressive or disciplinary approach, often shelling out lines when a quiet conversation would have achieved a better outcome. Indeed, her over-exuberant approach had often had to be reined in by a passing teacher.

Emily tried to make friends with the newcomer, realising she would not have any friends yet, but found herself rebuffed by the prickly Aileen.

It was not long before Aileen latched onto the brash Bruce Sparling who James had managed, in the most part, to avoid.

The year of 2019 was bit unusual, with the spectre of Covid-19, and resulting lockdowns the following spring. With most pupils having access to a computer and the internet, schoolwork was switched to being "online" and designed to be returned in like manner.

During this time, Emily won an essay competition, which annoyed Aileen as she had put a lot of effort into her script but came third. Aileen was actually in the same year as James and cast her eye on this handsome but very timid lad. *Perhaps, when he is a bit older*, she thought.

While Aileen had administration and organising talents, she lacked any artistic bent that Emily had, and therefore her character was not compatible with James. She did not realise that the bonnie Emily had her "chosen one", quietly being watched by her friend Fiona, who was in James's class.

Emily knew from just looking at James's paintings and drawings that he was a kindred spirit. But, being Emily, she wanted to become accredited in Pottery and Ceramics before having a steady boyfriend.

# Chapter 3

# The Tragedy

The previous year, James's father John was in charge of a group of forestry workers. However, with several of John Mackay's team of woodsmen being away ill, they got behind in the schedule of felling certain trees that, in most cases, were chosen because they would present an obstruction when felling in earnest was to start in a given area. Just occasionally they were asked to look out for a tree that fitted specific requirements for a local timber merchant.

In October 2018, they received such a request for a 50-foot beam. Obviously, a tree that tall, giving a straight beam of that length with no main branches that would interrupt the grain and may lead to twisting, was hard to come by. However, late that month one was spotted high up at the end of a forestry track. Fortunately, it was away from the Great Glen Way, so the forestry workers did not have to make any special arrangements for walkers — not that many were about at that time of year.

The tree they wanted stood alongside a couple of others, the larger of which showed little signs of life and appeared to have only one live branch. It had an unusually wide trunk but looked stable enough. So, they concentrated on how they might fell the 50-footer. They climbed the tree, using the standard technique of a belt going round the trunk and attached to a harness worn by the climber. He could then lean back and gain height by using spiked shoes specially worn for such tasks.

The tree was inspected as the climber went up, and importantly a rope he had been carrying was tied at about 70 feet above ground, where the first branch of any consequence was growing. The climber then returned to the ground and set the rope taught to pull the tree in the direction they wanted it to fall. Unusually, the tree itself stood in a dell about two or three feet deep. Therefore, a careful measurement was made, and the lip of this dell was found to be 73 feet from the tree's trunk. It was a bit like felling a tree in a giant soup bowl.

What concerned the woodsmen most was that as the tree fell, the top of it would probably hit the lip of the rocky cup-shaped hole first, which might cause the top of the tree to crack or even snap off. This meant there was a lot of careful measuring to ensure that the key 50 feet of what would become the timber merchant's required beam would be unaffected.

At that time of year, the light faded quickly and it was very wet and boggy underfoot. The ground where the tree would fall was cleared as much as possible. However, with it all but dark, they called it a day and left the tree standing with the rope still attached, although it was temporarily tied up at the foot of the tree where they could retrieve it in due course.

With their preordained felling schedule still not up to date, they decided to concentrate on that rather than rush back to the 50-footer. The timber merchant knew obtaining such a tree could take many months and had already warned his customer to be patient, as beams that size were hard to come by.

It took until the end of November for the felling schedule to be back on track. Then there was little action, as the first week of December was very wet with snow flurries in the forest, and the trees were often growing above 400 metres — that is on a mountainside, not just a hill. Any schoolboy would tell you that for a hill to be called a mountain, it has to be over 1,000 feet high.

On 10$^{th}$ December, there was the start of a more settled period, which gave time for the ground to dry out a bit. And although John Mackay's Jeep was four-wheel drive, he wanted to be confident he could maintain grip going up and down the often very steep tracks through the forest.

On Sunday, the 16$^{th}$ of December, just after lunch father and son were out walking. They were making their way to a stone seat that allowed young James to indulge in his favourite hobby — one that his father knew would be his chosen way to make a living. John was wise enough to realise that any kind of office job was not for his young son. If James could not get out into the woods and countryside, John knew he would feel trapped.

John had bought a length of old carpet, which he spread out across the large flat stone seat so they could sit in comfort. The seat, which was at the end of a forestry track, was not being used as part of the Great Glen Way. In fact, you could go no further than the seat, and this allowed James to spend over an hour carefully sketching the view.

James had drawn the picture as if he was a Golden Eagle, looking from above, out over the seat, and across the loch in front of them to the south-east. Two tiny silhouettes appeared on the seat, which his father realised with a smile were himself and James. As the light faded, they decided it was time to head home for tea. So, folding his sketch pad up and putting the fine-tipped black biro in his pocket, James stood up, took his father's hand and they made their way down the hill.

When they arrived home James's mother had been busy making cheese scones, as well as a chocolate cake. James showed his mother his afternoon's work, which he was particularly pleased with. He felt that with careful choice of colours he could give this picture the ethereal and magical atmosphere it deserved. In fact, he was already thinking it demanded a large piece of mount card.

His mother gave him a hug, as she realised that he had captured a magical moment with the two figures perched on the stone seat. She did not need to ask who they were; it was clear the picture reflected father and son enjoying a moment in the great outdoors together, and a smile came over Katherine's face.

James turned 15 three days later, just two days before the school term ended. As he went off to school on his birthday, his mother gave him a large tin of Roses chocolates to share with his few friends. Being of a generous nature, James handed one out to everybody on the coach, including the driver. As a result, the driver noted that there was little if any raised voices that morning, as the pupils chewed or sucked on their chocolates.

When he arrived at school and entered the classroom, James gave a chocolate to his teacher Mrs Morrisey and then to those who had not been on the coach.

Mrs Morrisey decided it was appropriate to sing Happy Birthday, which James had been afraid would happen. But he decided it was better he was seen as a friendly person rather than a quiet nobody, so he gritted his teeth until the last notes died away, then quickly opened his maths book and read what was the next part of the trigonometry chapter they were dealing with.

Back home, John Mackay had telephoned his crew to say it was time they got that 50-foot beam felled before the Christmas and New year celebrations. So, they headed up to the higher reaches of the forest. There was a stiff breeze blowing, but nothing that worried the seasoned forestry workers.

They arrived and set the Jeep where it could act as an anchor, attaching the rope to a winch at the rear to ensure the beam would fall in the required direction. The rope, of course, was already attached to the tree high up, where it had been placed some weeks earlier.

The normal procedure was carried out. A moderate cheese-shaped piece or notch was cut at the foot of the trunk on the side where it needed to fall. Then sawing with chainsaws started in earnest, cutting across the back of the tree. Every now and again the chainsaws were removed and the stability of the tree was checked. Eventually, when they were nearly up to where the notch had been cut, they withdrew the chainsaws. This left what was called the hinge — the part of the trunk not yet cut through.

If their calculations were right, the tree should fall forwards, closing the notch, and fall in the require direction. Just to help it on its way, they started to hammer metal wedges into the cut. This procedure should ensure the tree fell in the required direction. Indeed, after a few blows from a sledgehammer, there were a number of sharp cracks, and the tree fell exactly where they had hoped. Regrettably, with all the noise of their chainsaws and the concentrated effort of hammering in the metal wedges, they had not appreciated that a sudden squall had blown up and was now rocking several of the trees around them.

John, in accordance with the safety rules, had stepped back at 45 degrees, but behind where the tree should fall, about 60 feet away. Now he moved forward to measure where to make the cut to obtain the required 50 feet. So, he was looking at the prize tree and did not hear or see anything that might have signalled danger.

That's when disaster struck. The tree that they had ignored, appearing to only have one live branch, came crashing down and fell on John before he had time to move out of the way, pinning him to the ground. His workers immediately rushed over to lever the great trunk off John, but it had crushed his chest and knocked him out. By the time they could free John and try and get him to breathe, it was too late.

The group of workers, some in tears, could not understand how the removal of their 50-footer had meant the tree behind should be falling over without warning. Then they noticed that its trunk was all but sawn through. That explained why so little of the tree seemed to be living, and importantly why it should fall almost silently. A notch that should have been cut on the side, to show and ensure its direction of fall was obvious, was not there.

The strong wind which had sprung up was not that unusual, but then they realised that a couple of branches high up on this tree were acting as buffers against the 50-footer, which of course was now no longer there. Furthermore, moss and ivy growing up the tree had hidden any sign of a cut, and any piles of sawdust had long been hidden by bracken and other vegetation. They reckoned it had probably been cut three or even four years before and just left without any kind of warning notice.

Thankfully, between them the workers had pictures of both before and after for any accident report. But for now, they had to cope with the death of their boss. They carefully laid John in the back of the Jeep, and as they descended the hill, they made calls to police and the undertaker.

Richard Cameron, who was probably the oldest of the woodsmen, took it upon himself to go up to Rubha Ard and have the painful duty to advise Katherine of the death of her husband.

Poor Katherine was deeply shocked by this news. Pointing at the tea table with tears in her eyes, she told Richard, "It's young James's 15th birthday today." The table was set out with ham sandwiches and scones, and of course a birthday cake with 15 candles. There was also a large present from James's father resting on the chair where the boy would ordinarily sit.

Katherine looked at the clock on the mantlepiece and realised that in about 20 minutes James would be rushing up the hill to share his birthday tea with his father, who had promised to be there on time. Richard and the local policeman said they would stay to support her when she told James of the devastating news.

As expected, a short while later James bounded into the house, and asked why there was a police car outside. Katherine then took her son to one side and, with her arms tightly round the young lad, in almost a whisper explained his father would not be coming to his birthday tea as there had been a terrible accident.

James quickly put two and two together, with the policeman standing there as well as Richard, who he recognised. The boy fell down onto the sofa and began sobbing uncontrollably, muttering to himself, "He promised, he promised," as if his father should have been more careful and been home for his birthday tea.

Needless to say, it took some time to get James to compose himself. Katherine then handed him the present that his father had secretly been hiding for some weeks. It was a very fine large sketch pad and a smart painting set of oils, rather than watercolours. There was a very quiet "Thank you, Dad," and a few more tears shed before he carried his new artist materials up to his bedroom.

Later, Katherine persuaded James to eat just a couple of the ham sandwiches and drink a cup of tea, then suggested he light just one candle on the birthday cake. It was a symbolic gesture which Katherine thought he might appreciate. James, however, took one of the candles that stood on the mantlepiece instead, lit it, then pulled the curtains back and placed it in the window as if it were a signal to shine out across the valley and bring his father home.

The next day, James was dutifully up and ready for school, but his mother said, "No, son, I have rung the headmaster and told him you would not be back at school this term. It is only two days, and I don't expect you would have learnt anything of consequence. Mr Grant was very understanding and said that was fine.

"There is one thing you could do," she went on, "and that is to try out your new oil painting set, even if it is only the view from your bedroom window. Your father would appreciate that."

James ate breakfast slowly, looking at the empty chair where his father would sit, then he quietly went up to his bedroom and opened the oil painting set. He put a piece of A3 card on his easel and carefully first sketched in pencil the view from his bedroom window. The view was similar to the one from the stone seat a few hundred feet above the house where he had been with his father. This time, however, he drew two figures in a small rowing boat fishing out on the loch. It was a poignant reminder of an occasion when his father had taken him fishing about 18 months ago.

The painting took him all day, carefully mixing the oils to get just the right colours for the loch and the tree-lined banks.

Katherine left her son to indulge in his favourite activity as she knew it was his way of coping. She only interrupted him when lunch and tea were ready.

After James had retired to bed that night, Katherine peeped in to view the picture when he was asleep. Tears came to her eyes when she saw what was obviously John and James fishing on the loch.

## Chapter 4

# The Long Road to Solace

The spring term started on Tuesday, 8<sup>th</sup> January, 2019, and James was ready to board the coach as it drove into the hotel car park. As he stepped up and found a seat near the front, several of the pupils — particularly the girls — offered their condolences for the sad news. Indeed, there was an unusually quiet, sombre mood in the coach as it journeyed to the Academy.

As James alighted from the coach, his friend Lawrence stepped forward.

"I am so sorry to hear the news about your father, but whatever you do, don't give up your painting," he said. This was a wise and friendly comment by his one true friend, a boy James often played chess with.

Lawrence knew James was very close to his father from the comments he had made. Often, as they left school on a Friday, James would say excitedly that his dad was taking him fishing, or that his parents were taking him on the steam train to Mallaig, over the first viaduct made from concrete at Glen Finnan.

Over the coming weeks, James was notably more introverted. The teachers would often struggle to get anything from him if the subject invited a class discussion. But he did not ignore his studies, and his school reports at the end of term often showed slight improvements.

The following year, when Aileen arrived at the school, she found she was in the same year as James and immediately eyed the handsome laddie. But having heard the news about him losing his father, she thought it best to tread carefully and did not approach him.

The year of 2019 was a strange year, with governments caught out by the possibility of an impending epidemic, then in 2020 schools shut their doors with two periods of lockdown while the Covid-19 pandemic reigned. There were a number of requirements to try and reduce the risk of spreading the disease, including the requirement that pupils should wear masks. But by April most educational establishments were closed, including the Academy.

James was in someways less affected than other pupils who felt shut in and cut off from their school friends. He received his lessons by email and then he would send his work back to be marked, which worked well for a shy teenager.

It was not until the half term of the spring term of 2021 that the routine got back to normal. For James, this period of quiet reflection and encouragement from his mother meant he was much more positive in his outlook when he finally returned to school.

As far as sports were concerned, the restrictions were not so strict outside, and the Academy's hockey teams were back practising or even playing in matches. This meant the Great Glen Schools League reintroduced their annual competition that had been suspended in 2020.

The one thing that Aileen quickly gained a reputation in was her ability to score goals for the Academy's 'A' team. As the year progressed, they won the quarter finals and then the semifinals. The final, which the Academy had never won before, was played a week before the end of the summer term, on Thursday, 18th June, 2021. It was a close match, with both sides nearly scoring. But thanks to both quick moving and skilful goalies, neither side had scored before half time.

In the second half, both sides played a more defensive game, which Aileen felt was the wrong approach. So, as soon as an opportunity arose, she sped up the left side of the pitch, avoiding any tackles. She was a left-hander, which most of her opponents found difficult to cope with, and with just the goalie to beat, she flicked the ball over the stick and feet of the goalie, who had run out of the penalty area and was not able to kick the ball. Aileen then slammed the ball into the back of the net to loud cheers of her team as well as many onlookers. With only five minutes left to play, her team reverted to more defensive tactics and held out until the final whistle came.

Of course, Aileen was very much the girl of the match, and her achievement was duly acknowledged by the Head at the assembly the following morning.

Aileen was now thinking she should be rewarded by being made at least a Senior Prefect or to be chosen as Deputy Head Girl. However, Emily had already made her recommendation that the position should go to the hockey team captain Laura Thompson. The final decision was up to the Head Teacher and her deputy, but she always took on board the thoughts of the previous Head Girl.

Emily had quite reasonably pointed out Laura's natural leadership qualities and the fact that she was a popular and friendly girl. Aileen, on the other hand, lacked both these qualities; she was very much a loner and had few friends.

Aileen's antagonism towards the now former Head Girl festered and she looked for ways to upset 'Goody Two-shoes', as she saw Emily.

*

What Emily did not impart even to Fiona was that after school, when James had had an art lesson, she would sneak into view his latest batch of work. Emily by then was no longer a pupil, but being an ex-Head Girl, everybody knew her and did not question why she was there.

Most of the class paintings and drawings had little merit, but she could always spot James's work as it stood out from the rest as works with a quality that drew the viewer in.

"Do you keep these, or are they thrown away?" she asked the art teacher.

The woman replied that the pupils were welcome to come and take their work away, but few rarely did. Knowing this, Emily was able to collect quite a few of James's pictures.

At the end of the Easter term, there was a form competition in which the teacher put up a prize of just £50. James rather bravely submitted the picture he had so carefully sketched when he had sat with his father up on the stone seat, with the two of them sitting there and the view of the forest and across the loch. However, he made one poignant change, putting a shadowy silhouette of his father and just a touch of bright orange to indicate a hard hat.

Needless to say, it won the form prize and allowed young James to buy his mother a large bunch of flowers and a box of chocolates for Easter.

With the end of term approaching, all the teachers were trying to finish their pupils' reports, so the art teacher had just left the pile of pictures in a corner of the Art room.

Needless to say, Emily saw the pile and, assuming it was okay to take any she fancied, she took James's picture, which she stared at for some time. There was something special about this picture. *Who was the guy sitting on a stone seat?* she wondered. *And was it made up or somewhere special?* James had shown a beam of sunlight coming down and shining on the solitary figure. There must be something about this picture, but she could not quite make it out.

Emily took this A3 size picture home. As there was almost nobody about and she lived almost opposite the school gates, no-one saw her to ask what she was carrying. She had carefully rolled up the picture and placed it in a large tube she had brought along in the hope there was any art work worth saving.

Immediately she was home, she took it out and unfurled it to ensure it did not have any permanent bends. A few weeks later, she had it framed, and it hung above her bed for over two years, as she was now off to her ceramicist course in Edinburgh.

At the start of the summer term, when James came back to reclaim his prize-winning picture, it was nowhere to be found. The art teacher was most apologetic, saying she had not intended to throw that one away, but lots of rough work had been piled up and it would appear everything had been ditched.

Now settled on her course in Edinburgh – a year later than planned, due to the pandemic — Emily still looked on James as the "chosen one" and wondered how he was coping. She had confided in her friend, Fiona who lived in Inverbroch, that she rather fancied the almost 6-foot James, but did not want to approach him while she needed to concentrate on her course.

Fiona, who was slightly younger than Emily and therefore in the same year as James, reported that his name was on a list of a few of the most promising artists in the schools along the Great Glen, who were all being entered into a competition sponsored by North Coast 500.

Each young artist would need to produce a painting of any notable feature round the coast of northern Scotland. A list was given, mentioning such places as Eilean Donan Castle, the Coigach Hills, or the Smoo cave and waterfall. Although the actual subject was up to the artist to choose, it had to be a dramatic view that anyone driving past would seek a place to stop to appreciate — perhaps a strange mountain feature, or a place of outstanding beauty.

Emily was sure James would be in the running for one of the prizes, as all his pictures had the ability to stand out and impress the viewer. The finished art work had to be presented by 30th June, but the winner would not be announced until Monday, 19th July, 2021.

Happy that her wee "Claude Monet" was still practising his natural artistic talent, Emily was hearted to learn from Fiona that he was less shy these days. And she very much doubted he would have any kind of girlfriend by the time she came back with her hoped-for qualification as a professional potter and ceramicist.

The school term ended on Friday, 25th June, and by chance James was spending a few days the following week with his cousin Allan Mackay in Tongue. This gave an opportunity to sketch places that might be suitable for his North Coast 500 entry, including Castle Varrich which was one of the sites specifically mentioned in the competition. Once he was back home, he spent some time in producing a picture of the castle as his submission.

Although he did not hear about how his picture had done, he did read in the *Inverness Courier* that there had been over 500 entries. It was understandable, he decided, that it would have been a mammoth effort to write to all entrants to tell them that their picture had not been chosen. A list of ten pictures that would be used was published.

James, who could be leaving school when he was 18 at the end of the Christmas term, was not too despondent about the outcome. After all, he had won the form competition at school.

His mother realised her son needed to be a little bolder to get on in the world and manged to get him a job on Saturdays working at the Orange Berries Café. Katherine Mackay knew many of her neighbours and would often pop into the café just to have a chat with friends. Being a regular customer, it was not too difficult to get Mrs McCready to agree to take on James for a few hours on Saturdays.

The café owner realised how helpful it would be to have strong laddie about, who could shift all the heavy goods that would be delivered such as crates of milk and baskets full of loaves, along with big boxes of flour and icing sugar. She not only made cakes for the café, but also to sell at the local shop and post office.

James enjoyed working for Mrs McCready, and after he officially left school, he ended up working there six days a week. When they were quiet, he would sweep up the front of the café where odd detritus, often thrown out of car windows, would blow across the road and spoil the look of the place.

The local teen and twenties crowd were often found in the café on a Saturday and most days of the week during the school holidays. Initially they would tease the shy James. "Found yourself a wee girlfriend yet?" they would say. However, Fiona soon put a stop to that, quietly explaining that once was a joke, but they wouldn't like it week after week. "Anyway," she told them, "he is already spoken for."

"Really? Who then?" whispered a young blonde girl who was new to the area and had taken a shine to the handsome laddie.

"I am not at liberty to say," said Fiona.

When they would guess and suggest names to Fiona, she replied, "It is no good, I am not going to tell you. You will find out soon enough."

Fortunately, with Emily either being in Edinburgh or back home living across the road from their old school, nobody mentioned her name. That meant Fiona did not find herself having to keep a straight face or to lie to protect her friend.

Meanwhile, James was gradually accruing quite a lot of money in his savings account, particularly as he lived rent free and did not have any transport costs. Even on the minimum wage, his weekly take home pay was over £450. After the first month, he volunteered to give his mother £150 per week as part of the family budget.

The Mackays had managed to stay in the same house that they had bought 15 years before, as John had made sure the mortgage was protected by life insurance. On his death, it was immediately paid off, and he had wisely taken a further policy for £50,000 which provided funds for immediate needs, including a small Fiat car.

Margaret Macdonald, Emily's mother, had known Katherine Mackay for many years. They'd first met when James was only five and started to attend the primary school, because the Mackays at that time lived near the school before they bought their house in Inverbroch.

Margaret was employed by the school as a cleaner, and occasionally there was laundry to attend to. However, by the beginning of July 2023, shortly before Emily would be returning with her accreditation as a Professional Ceramicist (with distinction), a change was about to happen.

Margaret's husband, who was a plumber and heating engineer, had a business known up and down the Great Glen. But, with two grown-up children, they were finding their three-bed semi a bit cramped. Emily's elder brother George often wanting his girlfriend Felicity to stay overnight, particularly as she lived in Inverness — he'd got to know her when he had been studying there. When Emily was in Edinburgh, there was no problem, but when she returned George had to meet Felicity back in Inverness.

Almost magically, Margaret spotted an advert in the *Inverness Courier* about a house for sale in the grounds adjacent to a number of holiday lodges that had recently been built. The land owner wanted to sell the house to offset the cost of his lodges venture. But he also needed a person who could clean the lodges and do the laundry.

Indeed, he had been most insistent to the estate agent that he would only sell to someone who could do the cleaning work. The land owner felt the cleaning had to be done by someone living close by, so that there would be no problem if there was bad weather. He was prepared to pay slightly above the current rate, as the job was effectively only for ten months, with no cleaning required in January and February.

Margaret had hardly finishing reading the advert before she was on the phone to the agents, advising them that not only was she looking for a larger house, but pointing out that she had been a school cleaner for years.

"Where is this desirable residence?" she asked.

"Inverbroch," advised the agent.

## Chapter 5

# A Touch of Serendipity

When Emily's mother mentioned on the phone about the house for sale in Inverbroch, Emily was surprised to hear she would be living near her "chosen one". The new house had four bedrooms and two bathrooms as well as a study room, which at a pinch could be used as an extra bedroom, and was just what the Macdonalds needed. They always wanted to ask friends and relatives who lived down south, hundreds of miles away, to come and stay. When the children were very young, it was not too difficult to get them to hunker down together, but now they were grown-ups, it was no longer possible.

In the summer, the Macdonalds often travelled south to stay with friends who had four or five bedrooms, so the new house would allow them to return the invitation at last.

So, on Saturday, 2nd July, Mr and Mrs Macdonald visited their building society to ask how much they could borrow, based on Robert's income being much higher than when they had bought their current house. A few calculations were made and they were informed that the price of the new residence was well within their budget, even without the extra income from Margaret's cleaning job. This was fortuitous, as they expected there would be lots of odd extra expenditure to get the place right for them. But it meant when they arrived at the new house Margaret's cleaning job money would help pay for this.

When Emily arrived home a week later and saw the details of the house in Inverbroch, she could not quite believe how serendipitous this move was. She had been rehearsing various schemes to be able to accidentally-on-purpose bump into her braw wee laddie, but now all she needed to do was casually walk up to the local café and there he would be.

For months Fiona had been telling her, "You better get here quick, otherwise some wee lassie will whisk him away to her castle high up in the mountains." Of course, these messages were sent by email, so just in case Emily got really worried, she would add, "Don't worry, he is still yours. But will you be here for the ceilidh at Inverbroch Community Hall on Friday, 25th August?"

Emily replied, "I am not sure yet, but the agent is confident he will find a buyer for our existing house fairly quickly."

In the end, things ran very smoothly. It took just two weeks for a first-time buyer to turn up and say they would pay the advertised price for the Macdonald's house. The solicitors then got their act together and a completion date was fixed for Thursday, 24th August, 2023.

With a few short weeks before the move, Margaret had an opportunity to go to Inverbroch and see her new employer, Nicholas Cameron, who was quite impressed how Margaret quickly saw what was needed. She advised him she would need an extra-large washing machine if she was to cope with several sheets and pillowcases, not to mention large towels on an almost daily basis in the holiday season. She would also need a tumble drier, as the weather could not be assured.

Her employer could see how Margaret was thinking and quickly agreed to foot the bill for the new machines.

Surprised, but delighted, Margaret told him, "Don't worry about getting a plumber to fit them, as my husband is a plumber and heating engineer."

"Great," said Nick Cameron. "I may have some work for him soon, as I have just bought a large house up the road towards Inverness, and most of the plumbing is about 60 years out of date."

Over the next few weeks there was much packing and making sure all their electricity and water bills were paid up. They also advised the local authority about the council tax, which would be paid by the new owners from September.

*

At eight o'clock sharp on Thursday, 24th August, a large pantechnicon drew up and parked with its ramp lowered to align with the end of the Macdonalds' drive.

Like any move, it always takes longer to pack than unpack, particularly as there are always awkward shaped bits of furniture to fit in which can be quite fragile and cannot go under other items. But by 13:30, everything was packed and ready to go. The only items kept back were a kettle, six mugs, the tea caddie, and some milk, so that Margaret could give the removal men a well-deserved mug of tea. She'd also held back some still-warm sausage rolls, which she had placed in the microwave, as it was not going to the new house.

With the move only being seven-and-a-half miles away, the delivery and unloading could be done on the same day. So, they met Nicholas Cameron with the keys at the new house, and it did not take long for all the heavy items, such as beds and tables, to be placed in their respective rooms. Needless to say, piles of boxes of clothes and kitchen equipment remained unpacked but in the correct rooms.

Emily was pleased to have a back bedroom with a view over the loch. One of the first things she did was hang up her precious picture that had won James the art prize. Later that night, as she came into her room and looked at the picture and then looked out of the window, a shudder went down her spine.

There were features in the picture that seemed to match what she could see out of her window. She knew where James lived and suddenly realised that, but for the difference in height, she got a similar view.

The next morning even the assertive confident Emily hesitated before she said to her mother, "I think I'll wander up to the café and see who is about."

"Oh, young James Mackay works there now. You know, the braw laddie that painted that picture that is hanging on your bedroom wall."

"Oh, does he?" said Emily in a rather nonchalant manner and stepped out of the front door.

Her mother burst into laughter after the door closed; she knew exactly why Emily was going up the road. It had been obvious for years that this wee laddie had a special place in her daughter's heart. She was just surprised Emily had not made her feelings known months before, but equally she knew her daughter was determined to get her accreditation for ceramics before approaching wee James.

The morning was rather dull with a slight drizzle in the air, so Emily had the hood up on her coat. So, when she stepped into the café, she was not recognised except by Fiona, who knew sparks were about to fly.

Emily sat down opposite Fifi — as Fiona was often called — with her back to James. A few moments later he dutifully came over to take her order.

"Good morning, what can I get you?" said James, assuming she was another of Fiona's friends. After all, although James had known Emily when she was head girl, that had only been at a distance and over two years ago.

Emily did not immediately look up but said very calmly, "I'll have a flat white and a toasted tea cake, please, James. And just one more thing."

Looking up at her tall, handsome laddie, she added, "Would you like to take me to the ceilidh tonight? It starts at seven o'clock. And wear your Mackay tartan kilt, as it has various shades of green which I think is very suitable for an artist like yourself."

James was absolutely stunned. Looking down at this bonnie lass, he thought she must be the most attractive and beautiful girl in the whole of the Great Glen. He couldn't believe she was asking *him* to take her to the dance tonight.

Emily could see that James was slightly embarrassed, so gave him one of her smiles. "It's okay, James, I'll look after you. Anyway, they have a caller, so you don't have to know all the moves."

Pinching himself in case this was a dream, James finally got his voice back, swallowed, and replied, "Err, yes, but where do you live?"

"We have just moved into the big house by all those new holiday lodges in the grounds of Inverbroch Lodge."

James, still slightly dazed, merely replied, "Right," then hurried back to the counter to prepare the flat white and put a tea cake into the toaster.

Mrs McCready had been watching what was going on and had noticed that as soon as Emily started to speak, everybody else at the same table and nearby had gone silent. Even she realised something special had just happened.

What the group had not noticed was that the clouds which had been causing the drizzle had parted, and almost at the moment Emily had looked up and smiled at James, a beam of sunshine had come through the window, like a spotlight on two people in a play. Only Mrs McCready took a sharp intake of breath at this magical scene.

One other person who witnessed this divine event was Aileen, who had accompanied her mother for a morning cup of coffee. Over the previous weeks, Aileen had tried to strike up a conversation with James, but had never really got anywhere. However, as she was some distance away, she did not really hear what had been said.

When James moved away, Fifi scolded her friend. "You might at least have given him more warning. The poor laddie was almost shaking at the knees." Then the two friends burst into a fit of giggles.

"It's not fair," said a couple of the other girls at the table. "We were hoping he would choose one of us to go to the dance tonight."

"Well," said Emily rather mischievously, "you only had to ask. But you are too late, he's mine now."

The girls could see that messing with the new kid on the block was not something you did.

However, to lighten the tone Emily added, "At the ceilidh tonight, I expect you will all have the chance of a 'do-si-do' with my county man, but when the clock strikes midnight, I shall whisk him away to my castle on the hill. And woe betide any wee lassie that gets in my way." Then a big smile came across her face, and everybody dissolved in fits of laughter.

"You are wicked," said Fifi.

At that point James arrived with the drink and toasted tea cake for Emily and placed the tray down on the table. He proceeded to neatly set down the knife, then the plate with the toasted tea cake, with two butters and a tiny pot of jam, and finally the large cup of flat white coffee.

"Will there be anything else?" he asked dutifully.

"No, that's lovely, James. It looks great. Please pass my compliments onto the chef."

"Chef?" said James. "Err, that's me." Then he realised Emily was just teasing him. "I think Fiona is right; you are wicked," he said, which also confirmed he was not deaf.

With that the whole table erupted in laughter.

"You tell her, James," said Matthew, Fiona's boyfriend.

Then James, as if to show he was no pushover, said to Emily, "And, Miss Emily, I expect you to wear your tartan skirt, and I shall be knocking on your front door at ten to seven. Don't be late "

At this point, the assembled crew started clapping. Emily beamed, as she remembered he had been a shy teenager at school and she was pleased to find he now had a bit of spunk. *I think I have definitely chosen the right man here,* she thought to herself.

"Okay, James," she told him. "I promise to be ready and good from now on."

"But not that good," Fiona chipped in.

"Now who is being wicked?" laughed Emily.

"Okay, truce," said Fiona, and held out her hand.

"I assume you will be at the ceilidh tonight?" Emily asked her.

"Oh, don't worry. I would not miss this for the world."

Of course, Aileen had been listening intently to all this and was now rather aggrieved that Emily had captured the wee laddie that she fancied right under her nose. Immediately she began to ponder how she might get her own back. Her thoughts turned back to the Academy. Emily had of course risen to be Head Girl, while Aileen had never even been chosen as Deputy because the hockey team captain Laura Thompson had been awarded that post.

# Chapter 6

# The Ceilidh

At the Orange Berries café, by 4pm James had made sure all was tidy, and everything washed up and put in its right place. Then he said goodbye to Mrs McCready and almost skipped down the road home to Rubha Ard.

With a big smile on his face, he said to his mother, "I am going to the ceilidh tonight at the community hall."

"Oh, good idea. Perhaps you'll meet a nice young girl."

"Oh, I already have. Her name is Emily Macdonald. And, Mum, she is an absolute stunner."

"Where does she live?" asked his mother; she already knew but pretended ignorance.

"In that big house that has just been sold near the new holiday lodges in the grounds of Inverbroch Lodge."

"Oh, that will be Margaret Macdonald's daughter. She is a lovely girl. She's apparently been down in Edinburgh for the last couple of years doing a ceramics course, and is a very determined young lass. According to her mother, when she makes her mind up about something, there is no changing it. You are definitely the favoured one if she let you ask her to the ceilidh."

"Well," replied James slightly sheepishly, "actually she asked me."

"That sounds just like Emily, from what her mother told me about her." His mother smiled. "Well, your tartan kilt is all clean and pressed, hanging up in your wardrobe."

James tripped upstairs to get ready. But on opening his wardrobe door and finding the kilt and jacket as his mother had said, he wondered how she had known he would be wanting it that night.

*

At half past six, James stepped out looking very smart. Although the evening was dry and quite warm, he carried a large umbrella just in case.

Taking his time, it took him nearly 20 minutes to walk to the Macdonalds' house, and although he did not know if it actually had a name, he was a little surprised to see a hastily painted board announcing "Macdonalds' House". *A wise move to let the postman know who was now living here,* thought James.

He looked at his phone. 18:49. Counting to himself, he reached 55 then knocked on the door. It was opened by Mrs Macdonald, who James recognised from her days as the cleaner at school.

"James, how lovely to see you. And my, you look very smart indeed. Emily will be right down. Step inside for a moment."

A few seconds later, Emily bounded down the stairs and to his slight embarrassment gave him a kiss on the cheek.

"Let's go. Bye, Mum," she called back, almost dragging James out the door.

Hand-in-hand, they walked up towards and then along the main road, which initially had a well-trodden grass verge then a proper pavement.

Emily had her arm tightly around James's waist, and as they entered the community hall, he dutifully paid £14 for two tickets.

"The first dance is usually the Gay Gordons," Emily informed him. "It is easy to follow the moves, so just hold on to me, my wee laddie, and you'll be fine."

The usual crowd that James knew from serving in the Orange Berries Café were already there. Emily hugged Fiona and a few of the lads, which James felt a little awkward about. However, he re-established his place by her side by getting some drinks.

The first dance was indeed the Gay Gordons, and Emily grabbed her braw laddie and pulled him onto the dance floor, where other couples were already lined up. For this dance, you stay with your partner, although you may twist and turn, and then in turn dance to the head of the column. James had done some line dancing at junior school, which he'd enjoyed, so was not a complete novice.

At the end of the dance, they returned to the table where their drinks were, and as usual Emily took over the conversation. However, after only a couple of minutes, the Caller asked for two circles — lassies on the inside, lads on the outside. Before James could take the hand of his beautiful girlfriend, she was whisked away by another young lad who knew Emily, and she dutifully obliged. James, though, felt as if he had been abandoned.

Emily looked back and saw James looking slightly crestfallen. She wondered if he was questioning whether she had asked him to the ceilidh just so she could see all her old friends and was only pretending to be *his* girl.

She rushed back and whispered in his ear. "Don't worry, my little Claude Monet, everybody gets to dance with whoever you like. But the important thing is who you have the last dance with, and that will definitely be me."

Then she called over to Fiona, "Fifi, can you look after James for me?"

Seeing his slightly confused look, Fiona told him, "Don't you worry, Emily won't abandon you. She has been after you for years, and woe betide any young girl that tries to take you away from her."

41

James was puzzled by this remark. Plucking up a little courage, he asked, "What do you mean 'years?"

"Oh, I can come clean now," Fiona laughed. "While Emily was away in Edinburgh, I was keeping her up-to-date and making sure none of the other girls latched onto you. You are her 'chosen one', but as you will remember from when she was Head Girl, she made sure she was friends with everyone… except possibly Aileen Murphy, who seemed to think she should be at least Deputy Head Girl. Emily has plans for you, but all in good time, and don't worry, I am sure you'll be happy when she explains things further."

This last remark left James even more confused, but at the same time a little intrigued. While Fiona was bringing James up to speed, he was dancing, often swinging his partner or finding it was a do-si-do, so he wondered if he had really heard correctly.

Once the dance ended, he found Emily and asked her point blank, but in a whisper, "Fiona tells me you have plans for me, is that true?"

"Oh, don't worry. I'll explain everything tomorrow." Then she deliberately bent over and gave him a cuddle and kiss.

"Now, be bold," she said. "Get ready for the next dance, but I shall sit this one out, so you are on you own, my wee county man."

As it happened, they were asked to form squares of four pairs, so James plucked up his courage and went over to one of the young girls who had been at the café that morning.

The wee blonde girl was called Yvonne, and James asked her very politely if she would care to take the next dance with him. She practically leapt onto her feet, thinking to herself, *I am going to dance with the handsome James after all.*

At the end of what was the reel of the Royal Scots, both James and wee Yvonne were exhausted and pleased that the interval had been announced.

James sat down next to his beautiful Emily, looked across at her and smiled.

"What are you smiling at, my wee James?"

"I am still trying to decide if this is all a dream."

With that, Emily burst into laughter. "You're not the only one. After all, before this morning I last saw you over two years ago, partly because of the Covid epidemic. So, I am delighted you have grown up to be such a tall, braw laddie."

With that she cupped her hands around his cheeks and gave him a long loving kiss.

"You just keep dreaming, my wee laddie. Now, let's get some food; all this dancing has given me an appetite. In fact, why don't you get us some more drinks, and I'll get enough food for both of us."

As she went over to the tables where the food was being served, she found her mother there helping out.

"This is a tidy spread," she said.

"And how's your young partner?" asked her mum.

"Brilliant, Mum." Emily gave her mother a wink. "He thinks he is dreaming," she laughed.

"You be kind to him, Milly. He is still quite a shy laddie."

"Oh, not as shy as you may think, Mum." And she winked at her again.

With two plates piled with quiche, cucumber and tomato salad, couscous, sausage rolls, and an odd gherkin or two, Emily returned to where James was waiting with the drinks.

In the second half James was much bolder, feeling like most of the other boys and girls because he now had a 'partner'. He also felt more confident knowing that Emily said she was going to look after him.

By the way of a short interlude, before the final dance four brave lassies danced a Highland reel and were rewarded with a great cheer and much clapping. Then the Caller announced sadly this would be the last dance.

James immediately took Emily's hand, whispering, "I think this is our dance."

"Don't you worry, my wee laddie, I'm all yours from now on," she replied and promptly gave him a kiss on his cheek to seal her promise.

After the dance ended, James collected his umbrella and dutifully escorted Emily out of the hall. As they walked back to her house, they said very little, happy just to hug each other.

On arriving outside Emily's house, James said a little dramatically, "Are you going to leave a glass slipper behind, so I can trace you tomorrow?"

Emily burst into laughter.

"Oh, you are wonderful," she said. Then she opened the front door, stepped inside, took off one of her shoes and cried, 'Catch!' Blowing him a kiss, she told him, "If it fits tomorrow, I'll marry you!" And she closed the door.

James was left standing in the dark with Emily's shoe in his hand. He then slowly walked back to Rubha Ard, still wondering if the whole evening had been a dream.

When he arrived home, his mother asked how he had got on.

"She is lovely, Mum, but has a wicked sense of humour."

Katherine then noticed the shoe in his hand. "Why are you carrying a lady's shoe?"

"Oh, that's Emily for you. I said jokingly perhaps that I should keep one of her glass slippers so I can find her tomorrow. Then she stepped inside, took off one of her shoes and tossed it at me, saying if it fits tomorrow, I can marry her."

Katherine burst out laughing. "Well," she said, "you could do worse. Oh, by the way, I've asked some friends of mine to come round to tea tomorrow. It would be nice if you were here to greet them."

"Okay, Mum," said James and tripped upstairs to his bedroom.

Initially, James could not get to sleep. He kept looking at the shoe as if it might disappear, but eventually he drifted off to sleep with a smile on his face.

*

At the ceilidh, no-one had really noticed that poor Aileen was there without the brash Bruce Sparling.

She noticed Emily seemed be the favoured girl, with lots of men vying to have the next dance with her. She also noticed that young James seemed to be much bolder and more confident in Emily's company.

After the interval, she tried to catch James's eye and at least get one dance with him. But the best she managed was passing him as they 'Stripped the Willow'.

Wandering home on her own, she was almost in tears as she started to plan how she might get her own back. She grumbled to herself as she walked along that Emily seemed to get everything: she'd apparently won the Blue Ribbon awarded to the best student at her ceramics class for that year, which came with a tidy prize of £1,000. Aileen, on the other hand, had tried really hard at her school essay competition, but just got 'highly commended' and, of course, no money.

By the time she arrived home, she was not in a good mood and simply brushed off her mother's questions in an offhand manner, then trotted off to bed.

*Chapter 7*

# We're Sitting
# in the Picture!

The next day was Saturday so James was serving at the Orange Berries Café. Most of the usual crew called in, so the morning was quite busy. Fiona asked if he had enjoyed the ceilidh last night.

"Yes, it was great. I now know a lot more Scottish dances. We used to do line dancing at junior school with Mr Hamilton, who used to play the piano and taught us quite a few dances."

"Has Emily been in yet?"

"Emily?" said James, as if he did not know anybody by that name. "Oh, you mean that tall girl with the leaf green eyes."

Fiona smiled at him and quickly realised James seemed to have developed Emily's wicked sense of humour overnight.

"Well, no, not yet," he replied with a slight touch of disappointment in his voice.

In fact, Emily did not call in all day.

The afternoon was very quiet, so James was able to leave at 4pm promptly. When he got home, he had just sat down in the kitchen for two minutes when there was a knock on the front door. His mother beckoned him to open it and see if it was the mysterious friends she had mentioned coming to tea.

He opened the door to find Mr and Mrs Macdonald, and invited them to come in.

Initially, James was both confused and disappointed, as he could not see Emily with them. But just as he was closing the door, Emily rushed out from where she was hiding and stole a kiss.

Once she was inside, James composed himself and showed Robert and Margaret Macdonald into the lounge. Emily, however, hung back, and as James went back into the hall, she stole another kiss.

From the lounge, Robert Macdonald said in a loud voice, "James, before you do anything unwise with my daughter, I think you had better check her foot fits in that shoe you are holding from last night."

With that, all the grown-ups burst into laughter.

Emily shouted back, "Dad, stop teasing the wee laddie."

Robert was not put off by Emily's plea. "I think she is size 6, so if you find it is not a good fit, you have got the wrong girl." Again, everyone laughed.

Emily did not respond, but instead dragged her laddie upstairs to his bedroom, where she was about to give him another kiss. But James gently stepped out of the embrace.

"No, I need to check first," he told her. He took the black shoe from the top of the sideboard, removed her brown shoe from her left foot, then carefully slid her foot into the black shoe and asked her to stand up.

Emily did not object but just giggled slightly.

"It seems to be a perfect fit," James announced.

Then he stood up straight and looked down into Emily's leaf green eyes. "I think that means you can marry me."

Emily then took her wee laddie and gave him a proper kiss, saying, "Of course I will."

They sat on the bed for a few moments then James suggested they go out for a walk. "I want to show you somewhere special," he explained.

As they went downstairs and announced they were going for a walk, James's mother told them, "I am serving tea at six. So be back by then."

Arm-in-arm they stepped out and wandered up the steep Great Glen Way, moving east at the high point. After about 300 yards, they went down the path to the stone seat.

James had grabbed his rucksack as they left, which among other things had his sketch pad. Arriving at the large stone seat, he produced an old, large bath towel, which he spread out for them to sit on.

As they turned round to take in the view across the loch, Emily suddenly let out a gasp.

"The picture, the picture," she said. "I know where we are. We are sitting in the picture you did for the school competition." Then, almost in a whisper, she added, "Of course! The person with the orange hat was your father."

Emily gave James a hug and then realised he was quietly sobbing.

"Oh, James, you poor wee laddie, how you must miss him." She quietly rubbed his shoulder, drawing him closer to her.

James suddenly, tears still in his eyes, looked up at her curiously. "How do you know about the picture?"

"It's okay. It is hanging on my bedroom wall, but you can have it back. I didn't mean to steal it, but Miss Hodges said I could take any picture that was not claimed because they just get thrown away as she simply does not have room to keep them all."

James smiled. "No, you can keep it, so long as you promise to marry me."

Emily burst out laughing. "I think I have already promised that once today. After all, the shoe fitted, didn't it?"

With that, they hugged each other, and for a few minutes leant back to look across the loch.

"When is your birthday?" James asked her.

"It's 9th June," said Emily. "Why?"

"That is St Columba's Day, so we will call this Saint Columba's Seat."

"Oh," said Emily, "I feel honoured. But how come you know about Saint Columba?"

"Because we have Saint Columba's Well down near where your house is, and the other day I looked him up."

This time there was no flash of sunshine to celebrate the naming of the seat, but instead a distant clap of thunder.

"It's okay," said James, and from one of the pockets in his rucksack he produced an umbrella.

Although not yet raining, they made their way hand-in-hand back down the hill.

On the way, James said, "Hang on a minute. You said today you would tell me about the plans you have for me!"

"It's okay, don't panic," said Emily. "I think you need to take your painting more seriously. After all, you cannot work in the café all your life. You need to start earning some serious money. The paintings in the café have prices on them like £7 or £10, but if they were properly framed, they would sell in a gallery for hundreds."

"Hundreds?" said James, slightly bewildered.

"Your pictures are as good, or even better than those in galleries in Wadesburgh, where the prices on them might be £350 or £400, and the really large ones close to £1,000. But as well as needing to take into account the time you actually take to paint them and the cost of framing; you need to note that a gallery might charge up to 40% commission."

"Wow," said James. "I did not appreciate my pictures could be worth that much."

"The other thing is," said Emily, "you need a proper studio. And I need somewhere for my potter's wheel and a kiln."

By this time they had reached the driveway of Rubha Ard, it was dry, but they could see most of the rain was falling in the loch. This is something that often happens. A black cloud approaches, but the mountains each side of the loch seem to channel the rain clouds along the loch, so little rain may actually fall on the land either side.

As they stood on the driveway, Emily continued, "This garage might do at a pinch. After all, the Fiat takes up less than a third. Obviously, we need to put in some stud walls and perhaps build a stone lean-to at the end for a loo and wash basin, and a place to put my kiln. You would not need heating as such, because the Kiln would warm the place up quite quickly, once it is up to temperature."

James listened to all this and said, "Sounds good, but how much would it all cost, and wouldn't we need planning? "

"Actually, we might not need planning, but my uncle would say the trick is to get the local parish council on your side, as far as any building is concerned. My uncle knows about planning; he is a qualified architect as well as being an Estate Agent. I reckon we could do it for less than a couple of grand. Also, my brother works for a firm of builders, so I am sure he would help."

"Oh," said James, feeling a little more confident that it was doable. "I have about three-and-a-half thousand in my savings account."

"Wonderful! I did not realise how rich you are. Another touch of serendipity, I knew there must be a reason why I agreed to marry you!" said Emily laughing. "It's okay, it's okay, I do love you as well."

"You are being wicked again," said James.

"I know." She grabbed James's hand and began skipping towards the front door. "Quick, we have only two minutes before they will be sending out a search party."

James then put on his best BBC voice as he joked, "Here is the six o'clock news. A helicopter was used this afternoon to look for the wicked witch from the north. Reports of sightings of her were given as near St Columba's Seat."

With that, James opened the front door and they both almost fell in as they were laughing so much.

Katherine called, "Oh, you're just in time. Now wash your hands and then you can tell us what you have been up to."

As they entered the dining room where a tidy spread had been laid out, Robert Macdonald said to James, "I hope our Milly has not been leading you astray?"

"No," said James. "I think I have tamed the wicked witch from the north."

With that the grown-ups began laughing, and even Emily was beaming.

"While I may be the local witch, they have named a stone seat after me... well, almost," said Emily. "It is now going to be called St Columba's Seat, because my birthday is on St Columba's day."

"Ah," said Katherine, "we have St Columba's Well down near where you are now living. So, I can see James's thinking."

Emily was about to say she had a picture of it, but stopped herself and instead just smiled at James. She did not want to upset her wee laddie in the middle of tea.

Instead, she turned the conversation to the need for a studio for James. "Obviously only if you are happy, Mrs Mackay, but we have been looking to see if we could convert your garage where you park the Fiat."

"Sounds interesting," replied Katherine.

So, Emily outlined the whole plan, even pointing out how within the family they had all the skills and knowledge to make it a possibility. Even Robert Macdonald agreed that it seemed a sensible plan.

But he was at pains to add, "It will be up to Mrs Mackay. She owns the land."

Katherine smiled. "Well, I have no objection, but the key thing will be whether we can get planning permission."

"Leave that to me," said Margaret. "I'll ring my brother on Monday and see what he thinks."

After tea the two lovers were back in James's bedroom, searching on his computer for the cost of things like picture frames, or the cost to have paintings framed. They also looked at the price of a potter's wheel and a front-loading Kiln. Emily realised she would need to find about £7,000, not to mention the cost of clays and glazes. James's savings would be enough to get the studio up, but they need another touch of serendipity to get Emily set up as 'Inverbroch's potter'.

When it was time to go home, they quietly descended the stairs, realising they had set themselves quite a challenge.

"Have faith, my wee Claud Monet," Emily said as she was about to leave. "I may not see you for a couple of days, because I am hoping to be working at the clay works where I went to learn the basics before I did my course. They are right along at South Lewiston, so I won't be home before about 6pm at the earliest."

*

In the end, it was Thursday, 1st September, before the artist and potter got together, although they had been in contact, sending each other loving text messages.

Thursday evening was bright and sunny, so James wandered down to Emily's home at about eight o'clock, and they sat outside on a bench seat with a view of the loch, quietly canoodling.

Once James had released himself gently from Emily's grasp, he said, "Have you heard from your uncle regarding planning yet?"

"He said he will come over Saturday morning. But as you will be working, I'll be there to show him what we need, if that's okay with you and your mum?"

James looked down to see Emily was now wearing a ring on the third finger of her left hand.

"I don't remember you wearing a ring before," he said.

"Well," she told him, smiling, "I have agreed to marry you at least twice, so I thought I better show I am no longer unattached."

James was thinking he better make this union official but said nothing to Emily and just gave her a squeeze. Unobtrusively, while holding her long, artistic hand up, he tried to gauge whether his own finger was larger or similar in size.

"When will you be available next?" he joked.

"I will be available for consultation, my wee laddie, on Friday at about 7:45pm at the Inverbroch Arms, where I will be taking a wee dram with my brother George and his girlfriend Felicity."

"Okay. Am I allowed to join this small group?"

"Of course," said Emily, "as long as you come with some dosh, as I will not get paid till the end of September."

"First you steal my heart, and now you want all my money as well."

"That's not all I want from you, my wonderful laddie," said Emily, gently caressing him where perhaps she shouldn't.

"You'll be asking me to take a bite of an apple next," said James.

Emily laughed. "You're as wicked as me," she said.

James pondered for a moment. Thinking back, he remembered his parents had gone off for weekend on their own to celebrate their 10<sup>th</sup> wedding anniversary at a place at Cut Lake. He had only been nine years old, but had found himself staying with his good pal Lawrence that weekend.

"How about we take a short holiday?" he suggested. "I know a place we could stay, and it should be within our... well, okay, my budget. It is a rather comfortable shed."

"Shed!" said Emily, slightly disconcerted.

"Don't worry," said James. "Look, I have some pictures on my phone."

Emily looked carefully and then a smile came over her face.

"Actually, it looks rather cosy. I see it has all mod cons. I also see it has a microwave oven, which will be fine for breakfast, but an evening meal will be a bit of a challenge."

"Ah, that's the clever bit," said James. "You go up to the station at Spean Bridge and catch a train to Corrour. They have a restaurant there in the Old Station House. You need to book, of course. Then you catch the last train back, which runs about 9:10pm."

"You never cease to surprise me how you know all these things," admitted Emily.

"Oh, it is amazing what you can pick up, eavesdropping on conversations of people that come into the café." He paused briefly. "If we are meeting at Inverbroch Arms on Friday evening, would you allow me to take you out to dinner on Saturday?" he asked.

Emily was a little surprised. *First, he is planning a weekend away, now he is wining and dining me,* she thought. *I wonder what this is really all about.*

"That would be lovely," Emily replied. "Should I be wearing my best tartan skirt?"

"Of course, as I shall have on my Mackay tartan kilt."

It was now about 9:15pm and getting dark, so James said he had better get home as he had not bought a torch with him.

What he did have was a yellow luminescent belt he kept in his coat pocket. That would mean traffic should see him as he walked back along the A82, even though it had a pavement for most of the way.

With a cuddle and kiss, James left his lovely Emily, waving goodbye as he headed up the drive and along the road.

As he wandered home, he realised that he should be doing the honourable thing and asking Emily's parents if he could marry their daughter. He worked out that if Emily was leaving at 8am to get to South Lewiston, he could call at about 9 o'clock and be able to speak to Mrs Macdonald, even if Mr Macdonald might had left.

*

The next morning when he arrived back at the Macdonalds' residence, he found Robert Macdonald loading his van for a job in Inverness.

"What brings you here so early, James? I'm afraid Emily has already left."

"It's you and your wife I came to see," said James rather sheepishly.

Robert frowned. "Oh, what is this all about? You two fallen out already?"

"No, no," said James, "quite the opposite. It is just... well, I would like to marry Emily."

"Wonderful," said Robert. "Come here, laddie." And he gave him a big hug. "Margaret!" he shouted.

Emily's mother appeared at the door and saw young James.

"Guess what this laddie has just asked," said her husband. "He is willing to tame the wicked witch and wants to marry her."

Margaret gave James a hug and kiss on his cheek.

"We knew you two would be just right for each other for years, but now I am really happy that we were right."

James was rather taken aback by this statement but just beamed. He was pleased his request had been met with such enthusiasm.

"I am going to ask her on Saturday," said James.

Then he made his excuses as he needed to get to the Orange Berries before ten o'clock and waved goodbye with a big smile on his face.

# Chapter 8

# A Double Celebration

When James got home that evening, he said to his mother, "I think you said you were going shopping in Inverness tomorrow afternoon. Can I come with you?"

"Yes, of course," said his mother.

But James realised they would not get there until about 5pm at the earliest if he worked until 4pm as usual. "I will ask Mrs Macready if I can leave just after lunch, say by 2:15pm, so that will give us a bit more time," he suggested.

Katherine was guessing what James was going to buy, but simply replied, "Good idea. I am sure Mrs Macready will let you leave early. Friday afternoon is usually very quiet, and I doubt the teens and twenties lot will be around until Saturday morning."

"Oh, that reminds me," James told her, "I am taking Emily out for a meal on Saturday evening, so I won't want much for tea."

"Oh lovely. I am glad you two get on so well."

\*

The following afternoon James and his mother headed off to Inverness. On the way, James could not keep up the pretence that he was buying nothing in particular, so he confided in his mother that he wanted to buy Emily an engagement ring.

He asked if she thought a ring with green emeralds in it would be right for his new fiancée.

"I think that would be a very good choice," his mother said. "I notice she often wears dark green. I think we better get the ring first. The sort of shops I want will be open later, maybe up to six o'clock, but these jewellers might close at 4.00pm."

Katherine needed to go and buy some winter shoes and perhaps a scarf. She knew Academy Street was where she could find what she needed, but was aware that in the covered market off this street was a collection of jewellers.

Having parked the car, they walked along the indoor market looking through the windows of the jewellery shops. James was looking out for rings with emeralds and noticed several had a set of small emeralds around the top part of the ring. Then he spotted one with a large emerald which he thought looked really smart.

They went into the shop and asked to see the ring he had seen in the window. It was nine carat white gold and had a single large green emerald supported each side by diamonds. Reading the price ticket, he saw it would normally cost £715, but had been marked down to £549.

His mother said it was a good choice but asked if he could afford that much.

James replied, "This is forever, Mum, so I want Emily to have the best."

Katherine smiled and gave her son a hug. "I am sure she will be delighted."

Deciding on the size was the difficult part, and James thought back to when he had held up Emily's long artistic fingers. After trying it on several of his own fingers, he gave it to his mother. She found it was a shade small for her ring finger, but admitted her fingers were slightly thicker now than when she got married. The shop assistant was most helpful, though, assuring them that they could always adjust the size if it was too big or small.

In the end they plumped for a size 12, which Katherine could just squeeze on and felt would be alright for Emily's artistic finger.

"Do you offer insurance?" asked James.

"Yes, we do," advised the assistant. So, the relevant forms were filled in and the first year's premium added to the total cost.

They left the shop with the ring in a neat case, gift wrapped, and securely zipped in a pocket of James's fleece. Then they wandered over to M & Co where Katherine spent some time choosing robust shoes she was sure she would need for the coming season of frost or even snow. The shoes she normally wore in the winter months had seen better days.

While the shoes were being purchased, James wandered off to another part of the shop and spotted a nice warm scarf. It was labelled as a 'Breezy Day Space Dye Scarf', which he thought was appropriate. So, with the price reduced, James purchased the item which he quickly put into his rucksack. He had brought the rucksack along out of habit, and as always, his sketch pad was inside in case he spotted a view worth drawing.

Katherine had taken nearly half an hour choosing her shoes, so she suggested they head home without bothering to look at scarves.

"I can always buy a scarf from the craft shop at Inverbroch, if need be," she told him.

It was just after six when they drove up to Rubha Ard, and Katherine set about preparing soup with a tasty loaf they had spotted at a baker they had passed.

As James sat down, he handed over his secret purchase. "I thought you might like this, Mum," he said.

Katherine could not think what it might be, as she hadn't seen James buy anything other than the ring and the loaf. When she looked inside the bag, she was delighted.

"Oh, when did you get this?" she asked, wrapping it around her neck. "It's perfect. Cosy and warm, and a good colour to go with my winter coat."

"Well, you took quite a time choosing your shoes, so I wandered over to the scarves and hats part of the store," James explained. "It was labelled 'Breezy Day Space Dye Scarf', which seemed rather appropriately named. And as it was reduced in price, I thought it was an offer I could not refuse."

*

The next day was Saturday, so James was early at the Orange Berries Café, ready for the morning rush. The usual gang came in, including Fifi and Matthew.

"Will we be graced by the presence of the wicked witch from the north?" asked Fifi with a smile on her face.

James beamed but was puzzled how the news of his description of Emily had got out.

"She has not flown in yet, but I am seeing her tonight, so she may be at home."

"Oh," said Fifi. "Anything special?"

"Just taking her out for a meal," replied James, trying not to give the game away. But the big smile on his face made Fiona suspicious it was not just any meal out he was planning.

Conscious he might give something away, James quickly asked what they wanted and pointed to a rather nice coffee and walnut cake that had just been iced and set out by Mrs McCready.

Fiona noticed how James seemed to be avoiding saying where they were going, but said nothing. She did, however, wonder if he intended to pop the question.

Before he came back with their drinks, Fiona whispered to Matthew, "I think James might be getting engaged this evening."

"Wow, that's quick!" said Matthew. "They've only known each other for about a week!"

"So, when are you taking *me* out for a fancy meal?" she asked him.

Mattew was taken aback. "We have only been going out since Easter," he said, slightly disconcerted.

"That's five months. What are you waiting for, a better offer?"

"No. Now you're sounding like the wicked witch," said Matthew.

"It's okay, darling," she laughed, giving her beau a hug. "But don't leave it too long, or I might get a better offer." She giggled when Matthew playfully dug her in the ribs.

At that moment, James arrived with their order. "Steady, children," he said. "We don't want to spill the drinks."

Fiona and Matthew just smiled. But when the drinks and cake had been served and James had returned to the counter, Fiona commented, "I rather like the new bolder James. I think Emily has met her match."

"The wicked witch has probably mixed up some love potion and fed it to James without him knowing," joked Matthew.

"Perhaps you are right. The next time I see her I'll ask if she has any spare. Mind you, I could already have borrowed some and just asked James to put it into your Latte," Fiona added mischievously.

Matthew picked up his cup then hesitated for a moment before he was sure that Fiona was only joking.

As expected, Saturday afternoon was quiet, so James had soon completed his duties and was home by ten past four.

At 5pm his mother asked if he wanted to have a cup of tea and a biscuit or two just to tide him over until the meal in the evening.

"You look quite nervous," said his mother as he quietly supped his tea.

"Well," he replied, "it is not every day you ask someone to marry you."

Don't worry," his mother replied. "I am sure she will be all smiles, although knowing Emily she'll probably say no just to see the look on your face. So be prepared to have your leg pulled."

"I meant to tell you, I went and saw Emily's parents yesterday morning after she had left, and they were very happy about it. Mrs Macdonald said, 'We knew you two would be just right for each other for years, but now I am really happy that we were right.' Obviously, I'm not complaining, but how did she know?" he asked.

Katherine decided to come clean. "Well, you know I have known the Macdonalds since you first went to junior school. At that stage, you two never really got together, as she was of course a year older, and that is quite a lot when you are just five. But once you were both at senior school, young Emily confided in her mother that she fancied you. The fact that you both have an artistic talent appealed to her, but as you probably know, Emily likes things to go according to plan. So she wanted to leave school and do her ceramics course before she got to know you properly."

James smiled. "Oh, I see now why she always says, 'Don't worry, I'll look after you,' as if she has been planning it for some time. To all intents and purposes, she has!"

He drained his teacup. "If she does say no, I'll say, 'Emily, you've made a mistake. That is not part of the plan, and there will be no free flat whites until you change your mind.'" James joked.

He then went back upstairs to put on his smart Highland jacket and kilt, tucking the gift-wrapped ring into an inside pocket. Then he went back downstairs, looking very smart, ready to go down the hill to pick up his fair young maiden. His mother gave him a hug and bade him well.

After the door closed, she shed a few tears of joy and wished her husband had been there.

*

It was just gone 6:45pm when James knocked on the Macdonalds' front door.

"She'll be right down," Mrs Macdonald said, giving James a hug. "We've not mentioned a thing, but you know Emily, she seems to read minds. She has been hopping about all day with a big smile on her face."

James replied, "Well, if she starts casting spells, I have some garlic in my pocket in case of need." He winked at Mrs Macdonald, who smiled back.

"Ah, there you are, darling," she said, noticing her daughter coming downstairs. "This young laddie has been waiting very patiently for you, so you be kind to him. None of your clever tricks now."

"Mum, I'm a big girl now, so I have left my wand upstairs." Emily laughed.

Both James and Margaret smiled at this then the two lovers skipped out the front door.

"Where are we going?" Emily asked.

James stopped, temporarily unable to speak as he took in the beautiful vision in front of him, wearing her long red Macdonald tartan frock.

"Sorry," he said, "but you look rather desirable tonight." He cleared his throat. "I have booked a table at the Inverbroch Arms Hotel for 7pm... just for two."

Emily noted the 'just for two' and smiled, pulling him nearer to give him a kiss.

They walked along to the hotel, chatting quietly and holding hands. As they reached the foyer, they were greeted by young Yvonne, looking quite grown up with her long blonde hair tied back.

"I did not know you worked here," they both told her.

"I only started a week ago," she confided. "Have you booked?"

"Yes," said James, "for 7pm."

Yvonne examined the dining room table plan for that evening and indeed a table for two — number eight, which was in the far corner — had Mackay and the figure two marked by it.

As she showed them to their seats, they passed a long table set out for around 20 people, which left hardly any room for other bookings.

"It is for a diamond wedding anniversary," Yvonne explained, "A Mr and Mrs Gordon, and presumably most of their family."

They took their seats, and Yvonne handed them a menu. "Can I get you some drinks?" she asked.

Emily pondered for a moment and then said, "Do you have a Bristol Cream sherry?"

"I think we have," said Yvonne. Earlier she had taken a look at what was behind the bar, to try and remember what was available other than the popular drinks.

"That's a good idea to start with, to go with the *hors d' oeuvres*," said James. "I'll have one as well."

So, while Yvonne was dispatched to get two small schooners of Bristol Cream sherry, they studied the menu.

"I think I might try this Laphroaig cured salmon with horseradish ice-cream, pickled cauliflower, and hazelnuts," James said eventually.

"Em, I think I will just plump for the red onion tarte tatin," Emily told him.

"I never asked," said James, looking apologetic. "I assume you are not a vegetarian, or vegan?"

"Don't worry I eat anything... well, almost," Emily assured him. "After that I am going for the saddle of venison."

"Yes, I saw that, too," said James.

At that point, Yvonne returned with the sherries. "One of the proper waiters will take your meal order, as I need to get back to reception. The Gordons are due any moment."

Just then, a smartly dressed waiter stepped forward and asked if they had chosen yet.

"Yes," said James, I am having the Laphroaig salmon and Emily is having the red onion tarte, and we would both like the saddle of venison."

"Great," said the waiter. "I can get that order in straight away, as you see the kitchen is going to be rather busy once that large group start ordering things."

It did not take long for the starters to appear, and James raised his glass and Emily duly clinked hers against his.

"*Bon appetit,*" he said.

They did not say much as they ate, enjoying the first-class food. James felt they should at least have finished their starters before he produced the ring.

Meanwhile, the long table had filled up with much chatting and hugs as various people came in, most acknowledging Mr and Mrs Gordon with kisses and hugs.

Emily felt sure she was about to get engaged but tried to be patient just in case this was simply a meal and nothing special.

From the long table there was the sound of corks popping and what the two assumed was one of the couple's sons calling the group to order with a toast to their 'lovely parents and grandparents'." There was then much clinking of glasses and best wishes to mum and dad, or Calum and Charlotte.

When the noise subsided a little, James pulled the small gift box out from his inside pocket. Holding it up, he said very grandly, "My dearest Emily, this is the third time of asking. Will you marry me? But if either of us know of any just cause or impediment why we should not be joined in holy matrimony, we are to declare it."

The Gordon party temporarily stopped talking, intrigued by James's short speech.

Emily, meanwhile, had taken the gift wrapping off the case and gasped when she saw the beautiful emerald ring.

"Oh, James, it is absolutely wonderful."

James lifted out the ring and slipped in onto Emily's finger, delighted to see that it fitted. Immediately Emily stood up and gave James a long loving kiss.

Charlotte Gordon saw what was happening and beckoned to the waiter. "Please give the lovely young couple a glass of champagne."

The waiter duly obliged. "Mr and Mrs Gordon would like you to take a toast with them," he explained. "It is their diamond wedding anniversary."

James and Emily raised their glasses to acknowledge the kind gesture, then Emily dragged James across to thank the couple properly and to pass on their own congratulations.

Charlotte Gordon asked, "May I see the ring?"

Emily, still grinning from ear to ear, was happy to show it off to anybody, and particularly to the diamond anniversary couple.

Then, to the complete surprise of most of the Gordon table and especially Emily, Charlotte raised her right hand showing an engagement ring with a large green emerald very similar to the one now adorning Emily's hand.

"I am sure you will be blessed, my dear," she told her. "We have had sixty very happy years."

Emily, with tears in her eyes at such a magical moment, whispered that she was sure the Gordons would have many more years to come. Then they returned to their own table, where Emily again thanked James.

"Right," he told her more seriously, "you are not to cast any more of your wonderful spells until the dessert course."

Emily smiled and bent over to give her fiancé a kiss. "Okay, I promise."

James added boldly, "Now that we are officially engaged and both old enough to know better, we could take a weekend away at the 'shed and breakfast', couldn't we?"

"You never cease to amaze me, my wee laddie," Emily laughed. "A week ago, I was afraid you would be so timid you would not even take me to the ceilidh. Since then, you have agreed to marry me several times, and are now planning an illicit weekend away!"

"I just want to ensure we are compatible," replied James.

With that, Emily burst into laughter "Oh, you are wonderful." She continued, "If you are very good, I will give you the key to my chastity belt."

"Ah, you are not the only one who can be wicked," he joked. "I got a young pixie to steal the key, which is now safely in my pocket."

Glancing over to the Gordons' table, Emily said quietly, "I think we better tone this conversation down a bit. I am not sure who may be listening!"

The venison was served, and James asked for two glasses of red wine to go with the meal. The conversation then turned to the conversion of Rubha Ard's garage into a dual-purpose workshop.

"Perhaps we should set a timetable for the completion," suggested Emily, who liked things to be properly organised.

"I think we had better allow for the possibility of the weather preventing any work in December and January. And a lot will depend on whether we actually need planning permission," James replied.

"Well, according to my uncle when I saw him this morning, he thinks this will be classed as permitted development, but a letter setting out our plans should be sent to the planning office. He said it would be best if we advise your near neighbours of what we intend to do. The fact that I will have a kiln could worry a few people, as it can be hot enough to produce toxic fumes. But there will be guidance on what ventilation we need when we get the kiln.

"The fact that Rubha Ard is the highest house in the immediate vicinity should help disperse the fumes," she went on, "and they should be rising up towards my seat — or should I say, St Columba's Seat." Emily smiled. "I suppose, though, we should fit smoke and carbon monoxide detectors like we have indoors."

She paused briefly to eat more of her meal then added, winking at her laddie, "When were you thinking of checking compatibility?"

"I can see that the kiln is not the only thing that is getting hot round here!" laughed James. "Patience, my little Milly Molly Mandy. I think we should at least wait one hundred and forty-six hours!"

Emily was temporarily silent for a moment, thinking he had said 146 days, but after a quick bit of maths she replied, "So, the temperature should be rising by this time next Saturday?"

"Everything will depend on whether the compatibility chamber is available," said James in a slightly official voice.

Emily could not keep a straight face any longer and burst out laughing.

"I've got one of those temperature guns at home that we had to check people's temperature to see if they might have Covid. Should I bring it with me?"

"I think one of those watches that monitors your heart and pulse rate might be more appropriate," James told her with a smile on his face.

Having finished their meal, their conversation was interrupted by a waiter asking whether they required a dessert.

"Well, can we see the menu and see what we may have room for?" asked James.

So, the waiter passed them each a menu.

"I don't think I have room for the sticky toffee pudding, even if it is beautifully deconstructed!" said Emily. "I think perhaps a scoop of raspberry sorbet."

"Yes, it is a bit strange how you can deconstruct something even if it is done beautifully," James commented. "I think I will plumb for the bramble and vanilla cheesecake. However, I am rather pleased to be accompanied by a person who is very beautifully constructed, even if occasionally she needs cooling down from time to time with a little iced sorbet."

"James, you are priceless. Just remember I need a little personal attention from time to time to be in peak condition."

"Patience, my wee Milly Molly Mandy, your condition will be evaluated at the compatibility chamber, which is now in 145 hours and 45 minutes," James assured her with a twinkle in his eyes.

"Aw!" squeaked Emily. "Do we have to wait that long?"

"I am afraid so, but I will ring 'Shed and Breakfast' tomorrow."

Once they had enjoyed their desserts, James asked for two coffees, hoping to cool down his soon-to-be business partner.

"I have been thinking—" James began.

"I know," interjected Emily.

"Stop being wicked, and concentrate," he told her. "We need a business name for our joint enterprise."

"You mean like 'Pots and Paint'?" suggested Emily.

"Emm, I think there are probably other places with that name," James replied, frowning.

"You are right. There is one at Ferndown near Bournemouth," Emily admitted.

"Well, there would not be another Rubha Ard Country Wares," said James.

"That's true." Emily looked quizzical. "But does it describe what we are producing?"

"This is going to take some thought. And it would also be useful to have somewhere very local to have our wares on display, not just the café," James went on. "I noticed when I was walking home that the craft shop has a storeroom, with one side open to the pavement at the end of their premises. I wondered if we might rent it for a small sum."

"That might be a possibility, although I have not even been in the shop. Do you know the owner?"

"No, but I expect my mum does," said James.

It was getting late, so they drank their coffees and James asked for the bill.

They needed to pay at the desk at reception, where again they met Yvonne. James felt he should leave a tip, but how much? After a quick bit of mental arithmetic, he asked Yvonne to add £30 to the bill and passed her his bank card.

Yvonne said, "That's very kind of you, James."

Having processed the bill, Yvonne then handed them a note. "Mrs Gordon was most insistent I give you this note," she explained. "I said that if I missed you leaving tonight, I would be able to see you, James, on Monday at the Orange Berries Cafe. "

Emily opened the note written on the hotel notepaper and read it aloud:

*"Dear Emily and James, it was so lovely to share our anniversary with a young couple just starting out on their journey together. I feel sure the fact that our engagement rings almost matched will bring you joy. We now live down next to Loch Eil, a short*

*distance from Locheilside station, in Station House. I recognise the name James Mackay, as my daughter is a school governor at the Academy and was always commenting on the quality of the art work James produced. Of course, she also knew the name Emily Macdonald from when you were Head Girl.*

*"Do feel welcome to call in if you are passing. It would be lovely to see you again and know how you are getting on, as I could not help hearing about the plans you have for your joint business.*

*With best wishes,*
*Charlotte Gordon."*

"Oh, isn't that kind of Mrs Gordon?" said Emily.

"Yes. I nearly forgot, congratulations on your engagement. you two," said Yvonne.

Then. without prompting Emily proudly showed Yvonne the ring with its large green emerald,

"It was amazing that Mrs Gordon had a ring almost the same," Emily told her.

Then, with her arm tightly round the waist of her fiancé, they said goodbye and stepped outside.

When they arrived at Emily's home, she told him, "I wasn't going to ask you in — after all, we have had coffee. But as you are practically family now, and George and Felicity will have been waiting wondering if you were going to propose, I cannot disappoint them."

So, she opened the front door and pulled James inside. Of course, Felicity and Emily's mother immediately dashed out of the lounge when they heard the door open.

Then Emily announced rather grandly with a big smile on her face "Have you met my fiancé? This is Mister James Mackay; they named the county after him."

Felicity grabbed Emily's arm. "Let's see."

With a big smile on her face, Emily held out her hand to show off the emerald ring.

Both Margaret and Felicity said, "Wow, that's amazing."

Margaret added, "James, you wonderful boy, come into the lounge and let's have a small toast."

Robert Macdonald had heard all the commotion and had already put a few glasses out and was busy pouring a few drams of Glenfiddich Whisky.

"Right," he said. "We parents — and I include Katherine Mackay — have been quietly planning this day for several years. Yes, James, you may have only been planning it for a couple of days, but just once in a lifetime you see two people that are so obviously made for each other, that when this moment comes it brings tears even to my eyes. We realise that you two are still very young, but at the same time you are old enough legally to marry without our consent. However, as we have been wishing for this day for years, we can hardly complain now. So, we give you all our love and wish you many happy years of married life." Holding his glass up, he announced, "Emily and James."

Emily turned to her father with a beaming smile. "Thanks, Dad. I was a bit worried as to how you would react; after all, James is not yet 20. However, you will know I have had my eye on this beautiful laddie for a long time, and he seems to have grown up about two years since the night of the ceilidh.

James sat quietly, trying to take everything in then bravely asked Felicity, "Did you know anything about me and Emily getting together? Only, I am back to wondering if this is all wishful thinking and a bit of a daydream, and I'll wake up suddenly, after falling into a ditch somewhere and having knocked myself out."

Felicity took pity on the young lad and bent over to kiss his cheek.

"Don't worry, James, this is all for real, although from now on things may become a bit expensive!" She said this as she glanced over to Emily.

"Yes," said James, "I am beginning to find that. But hopefully my beautiful fiancée will be stumping up some dosh by the end of September, from working at the clay works."

James finally plucked up the courage to stand up and reply to Emily's father. "Thank you so much, Mr and Mrs Macdonald, for being so kind and welcoming. Now, it is getting late, and I must hand back — temporarily — your beautiful daughter for safe keeping, although I may borrow her during the coming week."

Robert Macdonald laughed. "You are welcome to take her off our hands anytime, and the longer the better."

Seizing the moment, James said, "Well, we might be away for the whole of next weekend."

"Yes, Mum," Emily chipped in. "Can I borrow your car for next weekend?"

"Of course, darling, so long as you drive sensibly and not while drinking. Do you intend to go far?"

"Only down to Cut Lake, near Fort William."

While Emily's mother and father where both intrigued by this request, they decided they had to start trusting the newly engaged couple.

But as Mr Macdonald stood up to show James out, he whispered in his ear, "I am sure you both will be good. And if not good, you will be careful." Then, gently tapping James on his shoulder, he added, "Give our best wishes to your mother."

James stepped outside, and with a friendly wave made his way up the drive and off to Rubha Ard.

*Chapter 9*

# Compatibility Gets Checked

It was Monday evening before James saw Emily again, and then only in the evening when she got back from work. She was borrowing her mother's car to get to and from work at South Lewiston, but instead of driving straight home she drove up to Rubha Ard and knocked on the front door.

Mrs Mackay answered the door with a smile on her face. "Come in and at least stay for a cup of tea. Of course, I would also like to see the ring on your finger."

Emily was happy to oblige, as she realised that all the Macdonalds had had the opportunity to celebrate their betrothal but Katherine had rather missed out.

"Oh yes, it is lovely and suits you well." James's mother gave her soon-to-be daughter-in-law a hug and kiss.

James had not heard the knock on the door but he recognised Emily's voice and bounded down the stairs.

"I did not know you were popping in this evening," he said, dropping a quick kiss on her lips.

"Well, I realised your poor mother had rather missed out on the celebrations, so the least I could do was call in and show her my beautiful ring," Emily explained. "Also, did you contact 'Shed and Breakfast'? And does your mother know you will be away next weekend?"

This all came out in one long sentence, so that James did not have the opportunity to respond. Once she paused, he replied, "Yes, I have mentioned it to Mum, and the wee lassie Ann, who calls it her chalet, said it would be fine for us to have the shed for the weekend, for only £160. She also said for another £35 she would cook us an evening meal, so I said if she could do us a meal on the Friday evening, it would be most helpful. On Saturday, of course, we can go off to Corrour Station House Restaurant."

"Great," said Emily. "I'll pack some stuff for breakfast — bread, butter, marmalade, etcetera. What cereal do you like, or do you have porridge?"

"I do like porridge, especially at weekends. Apparently, there will be tea and coffee available, and an initial supply of milk. "

Katherine noted how between them they got everything organised and smiled to herself at what a lovely pair they made. She listened as they discussed what time they should leave and what clothes they should wear, taking into account the expected weather. She noted decisions were made by consensus.

She did not mind that she wasn't involved and was happy to trust them to make the right decisions. *If they need to consult me, they will*, she thought.

Finally, James turned to his mother and asked if they had any maps of the area they would be visiting. Katherine was pleased to help, and from a drawer at the back of the lounge, she produced a couple of Explorer maps that her late husband had always kept handy when he was off to a new destination.

Emily stood up. "I must be going, or Mum will wonder where I've got to."

Katherine gave her a hug, adding, "Feel free to drop in anytime, even if His Lordship is not about."

"Okay, I might well do that. There are a few things I would like your advice on, but no hurry," Emily told her, then got in the car and waved as she drove down the hill to her home.

There were plenty of text messages exchanged during the week, but the couple did not actually meet in person until Thursday evening after supper, when they took a small dram at the Inverbroch Arms. Emily produced a checklist to see if they had everything, and she assured James she would fill up the car with diesel the following day, on her way home. She told him she was due to receive a little money for the work she had done in August, and she paid for their drinks that evening, as her father was giving her a small allowance for the time being.

*

On Friday at 5:35pm, the excited youngsters set off for the journey of about 40 miles. Emily, quite wisely, carefully kept below the speed limit and they arrived by 6:50pm. This allowed time for them to be shown their cosy abode by their host Ann, who also informed them that dinner would be served at 7pm. She told them just to come round to her house as soon as they had settled in.

It was a new experience for both Emily and James to be invited to dinner without any parent being about. When they arrived a short time later, the table was set for four, and they were joined by Ann's husband Robert.

He asked if they would like some wine. "We are having poached salmon," he said. So, they both elected for a glass of white wine.

Having taken their seats, the starter was a small bowl of rather tasty cream of mushroom soup.

Initially, the young couple were both rather shy, not saying a lot. But Ann had one of those warm smiles, like Emily, so it was not long before they were explaining all about their plans for a joint workshop.

Robert said if they needed any help with electrics, he would be happy to drive up to Inverbroch. "I am currently working on a house for a Nicholas Cameron near there."

"Oh," said Emily, surprised. "That's the person who owned the house we have just moved into."

"It's a small world," said Robert.

"My father might be doing some plumbing work for him soon, in a big house that seems to be still back in the nineteen-fifties," Emily went on.

"Sounds like the same house I am working on," Robert agreed. "I know there is a lot of plumbing work about to be done, and I need to rewire the whole house. I am making provision for washing machines and dishwashers which, of course, hardly existed in the fifties. Perhaps I'll meet your father in the coming weeks, what's his name?"

"Robert Macdonald," replied Emily.

He laughed. "That could be interesting — two Roberts in the same house. I'll need to be careful I don't electrocute someone if there's a shout to turn it on and they mean the water not the power. These days, I ensure there are surge trips, so you would only get a minor shock, but best not to have one at all. When I started, I did have a minor shock fitting a light socket where I had thought the power was off. Turned out I had pulled out the wrong fuse. It was an old house, which still had the old 15amp sockets. These days I check everything before I touch it. "

Ann interjected, "Robert, I think these young things have not come here for a lesson on electrics." She turned to them. "That reminds me, the Wi-Fi password for you is *chalet123*."

The bowls were cleared away and the poached salmon served.

"This is lovely," said Emily. "We feel very privileged to be wined and dined. Have you lived here long?"

"Over 40 years now," replied Ann. "I love it. Bedminster, where I grew up before we got married, is a nightmare for driving through or parking these days, and now there is ULEZ as well. Fortunately, we only have to cope with it on the rare occasions we go south to see relatives. Here, if you get more than a dozen cars in the same place, it's called a traffic jam. As we are of course on the Great Glen Way, we get more walkers than cars, which means a natural demand for B&B. Most people opt to have an evening meal, and as I love cooking it suits me fine."

"I am afraid James has yet to taste my efforts at cooking," said Emily, as she glanced up at James.

"I am sure Ann would be willing to give you a few lessons on the art of cordon bleu cooking," James laughed, and the two women joined in.

"You would be very welcome to come by for a few lessons," said Ann, "but not next week, as I am busy with Harvest Suppers."

Robert interrupted briefly to offer everyone more wine, which was accepted by both Emily and James.

Taking a small sip from his glass, James bravely turned the conversation to his paintings.

"We need to start making some real money, as we are both living with our parents at the moment," he explained. "So, I have been in contact with a gallery in Fort William, which sounds hopeful. He only charges 30% commission, which apparently these days is quite cheap. But it occurred to me that I could make greeting cards out of some of my pictures, and if you order at least 100 at a time, you can get the cost down to about 48 pence each — that includes the cellophane sleeve and an envelope. I never appreciated it before, but most shops charge at least £2.50 each, so if I sell them myself, I'll make £2 a card. Although I may price them at just £2 to give me a competitive edge."

Emily let James talk in order to give him encouragement, even though some of the ideas had been hers. Then she added, "It will be easier for James to get the money rolling in than me, as I have not even got the money for a kiln yet, and we first need to get the workshops up and running."

While James and Emily were conversing, Ann just listened and noted how they interacted. Although they didn't look old enough to be betrothed, she felt there was something rather magical about their relationship. She had met hundreds of couples over the years while running the B&B and could instantly detect any strained relationship; sometimes, she even wondered if divorce papers would be issued before the couple left and paid the bill.

These two, though, were just a friendly loving couple. Ann, of course, had no idea that Emily had been almost stalking her prey for a long time; how they had been like two magnets hanging side by side for years, then came a small gust of wind and they snapped together. Now, wild horses would not drag them apart.

The dessert was an Eton mess, with strawberries and a lot of cream as well as some vanilla ice cream. Finally, they adjourned to the sofa for a cup of coffee.

It was gone half nine before they took their leave and returned to the shed.

As Ann showed them out, she warned, "Occasionally, we get a couple of foxes barking and playing about on the lawn. But I doubt you will hear anything, as the walls are well insulated, and of course the windows are double glazed."

As Emily opened the door to the shed, she asked James cheekily, "Do you think she knew there would be some compatibility checking going on and was telling us that any screams of delight will be lost in the wind?"

"Well," James replied, with a big smile on his face, "let's see what we can do about that!"

*

It was just getting light, at about 7:20am, when Emily rose, took a shower, and then very efficiently organised breakfast.

At about ten to eight she called to James to put something on and come and sit at the table as his porridge was ready. To ensure James would not be disappointed, she had made sure to bring cream, sugar, and even some honey.

James wandered across and sat down with nothing but a bath robe on, rubbed his eyes, looked at the bowl before him, then at his beautiful fiancée. "Well, this certainly gets the gold star. Thank you, my love. 'Porridge piping hot with cream on, how they loved it. weren't they glad.'

"It's okay," James continued, "I am quoting from *Lost at the Fair*. It was one of my favourite story books when I was wee laddie and still at nursery school."

Emily laughed, "I am glad my first efforts at cooking for you have met with such enthusiasm. There are chipolata sausages with a tomato and some scrambled egg being cooked and will be ready very shortly. So, tuck in."

After a rather lazy breakfast, James rang the restaurant at Corrour and booked a table for 6:30pm that evening. At this time of year, it would be unlikely to be full, but he wanted to make sure Emily would not be sitting on the platform saying she was starving.

It was gone nine before James went off to have a shower and get dressed. Once he was ready, he looked at the map his mother had provided and noted the museum that Ann had mentioned, about 2.5 miles away along Loch Lochy.

"Let's walk along to the museum," he suggested. "Apparently there are loos there, and according to the website they seem to do drinks as well as sell ice cream."

So, having donned walking shoes, they strolled the few hundred yards to the swing bridge that crossed the canal.

But when they suddenly noticed a lot of black clouds overhead, they returned to pick up the car. When they arrived at the swing bridge again, they needed to hurry across, as it was about to be opened to allow a yacht to pass along the canal.

As expected, after driving just over two miles, a clear sign directed them to Clan Cameron Museum, so they parked the car and wandered in. The entrance fee was a very reasonable £4 each, which James duly paid.

As they wandered around the exhibits, they noted that the 'Gentle Locheil', the then Cameron clan chief, had given his support to Prince Charles at the Jacobite rebellion of 1745; regrettably, this would have been at some cost.

Emily noted the red tartan of Cameron was similar to her Macdonald tartan skirt. She was also intrigued by the piece of wedding cake from April 29th, 2011, when Prince William married Katherine Middleton to become Duke and Duchess of Cambridge.

The museum included a great deal about the Commandos, as their training had taken place here, establishing themselves in a big building further along from the museum, called Achnacarry.

The couple read and admired the many exhibits for over an hour, then went outside to sit in the sunshine on a convenient bench seat.

James, almost out of habit, took out his sketch pad to draw the view across the well-kept grass lawns to the River Arkaig. The area was park land, with several spaced-out trees, most being oak. James made a note that there were some rhododendrons in the distance, as this would allow him to add some red and pink to liven up the picture later.

Emily snuggled up beside him, resting her head on his shoulder. She was fascinated how James went about recording the scene; first, putting tiny marks where say a tall tree was, or a distant building might be. If there were stone walls, he often put just a few stones down, and once he felt he had the correct scale and position, he would add the rest. This meant if he needed to bring it forward and backward to get the perspective right, he could do so with a few extra stones, or perhaps hide the end of the wall behind bushes if it was clearly in the wrong place. Notes would be added: *pink R for the* rhododendron, or *light gn* for the grass. Just to one side, being just in view, he drew the old cannon parked near them.

It was now about 12:30, and Emily piped up, "I am starving. I feel I want more than an ice-cream."

"In that case, you had better prepare lunch. It is all in my rucksack," said James.

"Really?" squeaked Emily and dived into the sack. "A loaf, baby tomatoes, some pate, two plates and a couple of knives, a chunk of cheese, and even some butter. And what this? Looks like chocolate rolls! Wonderful, darling."

It was not long before she had cut several slices off the loaf and spread butter and the pate onto them. She placed the bread on the plates, adding some of the baby tomatoes and a few small squares of cheese. The chocolate rolls she kept back for the time being.

"Lunch is served," she announced.

As she started to eat, she leant across to James and whispered, "You were rather wonderful last night."

"You weren't bad yourself," replied James idly, as he concentrated finishing his sketch.

"Not bad!" shrieked Emily.

"Okay, okay, you were stupendous. But, my dearest, I am trying to finish this sketch before I get pate on my fingers."

"Sorry, my lovely," said Emily. "I think we need some more practice tonight."

"Practice? You seemed to have everything down to a fine art last night," James commented.

"I wonder how many positions there are in *Karma Sutra*," said Emily.

"About a hundred, I think, but it has not been my bedtime reading lately," laughed James. "We can discuss this further at another time, though, otherwise I will have to get the bromide pills out."

Emily giggled. "Okay, I'll change the subject. What time is the train from Spean Bridge?"

"I think it is about 17:50pm, so to ensure we are on time I think we need to leave about 17:20pm."

They relaxed in the warm sunshine as they ate, and Emily even fell asleep for a short time. When she eventually woke up, James suggested they wander over to the river's edge. This allowed him to make another quick sketch. The river was quite wide at that point, so he only had to make a brief sketch of the trees on each side. They then wandered back to the car and drove back to their temporary abode.

It was about 3:45pm when they arrived back, and Emily made them a cup of tea and put out a couple of the cholate rolls.

"I've been wondering about the work of illustrators," said James. "I am not into digital graphic designs, but I could do commissions for perhaps book covers that need a country scene."

"Good idea," agreed Emily. "You could put an ad in the *Inverness Courier*."

They finished their tea, and Emily lay down on the bed and fell asleep. James, on the other hand, got out his sketch pad and viewed his morning's work, adding some extra details here and there — a few deer crossing the park land, and in the river picture ripples in the water to give some movement to the scene.

At about a quarter past five he leant over and kissed his fiancée. She woke sleepily, mumbling, "Do you want me now then?"

"No, we don't have time," he replied. "It is gone 5:15pm, so we need to be away up the valley to Spean Bridge."

"Don't be cross with me, my angel," said Emily.

"I am not, but this is becoming like an episode of *Sex and the City*." Then, in a slightly exasperated tone but with a big smile on his face, he added, "There is a time for making love, and then there is a time for making love again, but I am afraid we need to eat first. So put your shoes on and be standing by the door in five minutes."

"Yes, oh master, your wish is my command," said Emily, smiling back.

At 5:20pm they jumped into the car and left the gate open, as they would be returning later. It actually only took 19 minutes to reach the car park at Spean Bridge, then they crossed over the bridge as the down service was on the far platform, No. 2.

The train arrived a minute early and, having boarded, the conductor came along for them to buy their tickets. Looking at these two young people, he asked, "Do either of you have a student rail card?"

"Yes," squeaked Emily, who had forgotten about using it. So, after deducting one-third, James only had to pay £21.98 for the two return tickets.

They stopped briefly at three stations, then it was quite a distance along Loch Treig before they arrived at Corrour. The conductor had explained that only the door at the end of the carriage they were in would open.

So, at 6:27pm they alighted onto the platform and found their way across the tracks to walk up to the Station House.

Inside there were a number of heavy wooden tables. None were marked as reserved, so they chose one to the side, as there seemed to be few dining that night. James went over to the bar and ordered a pint of Glen Spean ale, and for Emily an Elderflower Prosecco.

They then studied the menu and decided to skip the starters and go straight onto the Corrour venison casserole. The description explained that the venison had been slow cooked for 14 hours, so was very tender, and was served with mash and broccoli.

When the meal came, there was a lot of it, so they were pleased they had skipped the starter. They both then had the chocolate fudge brownie and vanilla ice-cream. As they had plenty of time before returning for their train, they opted for a coffee, Emily taking hers black.

As they drank their coffee, they pondered on when they might get the workshop up and running, and of course when they might get a place of their own.

"We cannot be down to the shed every week," said Emily, with a big smile on her face.

At five to nine they paid the bill and walked back across the tracks to catch the train from the same platform. As the train came, in the lady conductor opened the single door and welcomed them aboard.

Of course, it was now dark, and being out in the middle of the moors with almost no buildings, there was little to see till they arrived at Tulloch station. They then ticked off the stations — Achluachrach, Roy Bridge, and finally their destination, Spean Bridge.

It was then a quick drive home to the shed. As they entered, they noted all the washing up had been done and plates and cups put away. They also noted that the night was quite cool.

As Emily climbed into bed, she said, "Oh super, a lovely hot water bottle."

"Oh, I'm not hot enough for you then?" asked James cheekily.

"I'll let you know in the morning," she replied with a giggle.

*

Next morning, they rose quite early and Emily dutifully made James a bowl of porridge, followed by scrambled egg on toast. Then, having showered and dressed, they set about making sure everything was neat and tidy before they left.

By 9:45am they were almost ready to set off, so they packed the car then knocked on the door of the big house to thank Ann and Robert for making them so welcome.

"Come in," said Ann. "Can I get you a cup of coffee, or tea?"

So, feeling they could not refuse, and they were in no hurry to get home, they accepted her invitation and sat on the sofa.

James bravely showed Ann his sketches from their visit to the Cameron Museum.

Ann looked very interested. "I might buy that one," pointing to his sketch of the river, "once you have painted it up. How big will you be making it?"

"Well," said James, "probably about two feet tall and 18 inches wide, as it needs to be portrait-orientated for this subject. I can make it bigger if you like, though. Where were you thinking of hanging it?"

Emily smiled and realised James was cleverly asking questions that almost guaranteed this would be a commission, and he could reasonable charge say £275 for it. After all, there would be no cut coming off to a gallery.

Ann pointed to a large expanse of blank wall. So, James rose to imagine how his picture might fit.

"Actually, the river there is quite wide, so perhaps a landscape picture may fit better," he explained. "It looks narrow in my sketch but that was merely to fit the basics on the page."

Ann pondered for a moment and then said, "Yes, I can see what you mean. When would you be creating this picture, and of course I would need it framed? And how much would you be charging?"

"I think about £250," James announced bravely.

"That would be fine," Ann agreed. "Send me an email when it is ready, but there is no hurry."

It was nearly eleven before they said their final farewells, and the couple waved happily as they drove down the drive and then up to the A82.

They both felt a magical weekend was drawing to a close, so Emily deliberately drove quite slowly, saying very little till they had passed Invergarry.

Realising how she might keep the magic spell going a little longer, she said, "I know a nice place we can stop for lunch; it is called the Boat House. It's near the Lighthouse at Wadesburgh."

James leant back in his seat. "Well, my lovely Milly Molly Mandy, you seem to have thought of everything. Even the night-time entertainment was outstanding, even if it did need audience participation."

Emily laughed, blushing a little. "Oh James, you are wonderful, but I think the dexterity and prowess you showed could not come from mere audience participation."

"This is becoming like *Sex and the City* again!" James smirked.

At that point Emily squealed from fright as she quickly corrected her steering and briefly put the brakes on.

"Sorry, darling, I seem to have let my speed build up a bit, and that bend was sharper than I thought," she apologised. "When questioned by police about the accident, I would say I was only making love to my beautiful fiancé, and that's not against the law, is it?"

"And when the constable tells me off for driving without due care and consideration — doing over 50 in a 30 limit — I would assure him I was very careful, but did not know I was that hot!"

"Emily, concentrate!" James warned. "You are being very wicked again."

Fortunately, at that point they had reached the car park at Wadesburgh.

As Emily parked the car, she explained, "We need to walk, but it is only about 400 yards."

So, they crossed back over the canal, coming out near the lighthouse to find the Boat House. Although popular, it still had room for them at a table for two in the middle. They both decided to have a small glass of red wine with the beefburger, chips, and salad.

They ate slowly, hardly saying a word, and decided not to have any sweet dish.

"I expect there will be tea and cake when we get home," said Emily.

"Chocolate cake, if you drop me off first," replied James.

"That sounds like an offer I cannot refuse," Emily laughed.

They returned to the car hand-in-hand to drive the remaining 7.5 miles home.

"It has been a really lovely weekend, and I promise to pay for the next trip away," Emily assured him. "It could be at Inverness, because when Felicity is down here with George, her flat is empty and she is happy for us to use it in her absence."

"Sounds promising," said James.

A few minutes later, they were driving up to Rubha Ard, parking the car further up the drive than normal as it seemed George had already been busy with a digger.

When James opened the front door, his mother was waiting, having heard the car drive up.

"Come in, you two. Have you time for tea and chocolate cake, Emily?" asked Katherine, giving her soon-to-be daughter-in-law a hug.

"I was warned there could be chocolate cake on offer, so we skipped the dessert at lunch," Emily told her with a smile. "We stopped at the Boat House; do you know it?" said Emily.

"Yes, I have been there a couple of times. I think the last time was with your mother, funnily enough." Katherine went on, "So, what have you been up to? James said something about going to a restaurant where you had to go by train."

"Yes," said Emily, "it was a nice evening out, a relaxing train journey, and it did not cost us too much as my student rail car was still valid which meant one-third off. We had the Corrour venison casserole, which was very tasty. Apparently, the venison was apparently slow cooked for 14 hours, which meant there was very little chewing required."

Emily did most of the talking and after drinking his tea and devouring a piece of cake, it was not long before James fell asleep on the sofa.

Emily whispered to Mrs Mackay, "Let me help with the washing up" and she grabbed some of the cups and teapot and moved out into the kitchen.

"Mrs Mackay—" Emily began.

"Oh, do call me Katherine. You are family now," interjected James's mother.

Emily smiled and continued, "I've had a wonderful weekend away, but what I cannot get over is James. I am not complaining, it is just from what he used to be — a very shy, almost naïve young laddie — overnight he is now a very grown up, charming, confident braw laddie."

Katherine laughed. "Well, first the job of serving at the Orange Berries Café definitely brought him out of his shell, and remember, you had not seen him for over two years. But the night he came home after taking you to the ceilidh, he seemed to be a different boy. You must have put one of your spells on him.

"I think once he realised you were for real and that he had his own girlfriend, he felt part of the group. He was no longer on his own but now had you at his side. You have definitely had a very good influence on him. I think he suddenly realises he has a future with a very lovely lady."

Emily glowed. "Well, I had better not break the spell then."

At that moment, James wandered into the kitchen. "Oh sorry, it has been a busy day... well, weekend actually," he said apologetically.

"It's okay, my lovely, but I must go now. as I expect my mother is dying to know all about our weekend away."

Noticing that James looked slightly worried, Emily whispered, "Don't worry, my wee Claude Monet. What happens in the shed stays in the shed.' Then she quickly added out loud, "Have you told your mother about the commission of the river picture?"

"Eh, no, not yet."

"Well, I'll leave you to give her the details." And with a loving kiss, Emily opened the front door and was away.

## Chapter 10

# Is it All Too Good to Be True?

Monday morning and James was up — perhaps a few minutes later than usual — quietly daydreaming, imagining he was having a good morning kiss from his beloved.

His mother had put out the Weetabix, and as James wandered into the kitchen, he had a look of disappointment on his face.

"Porridge piping hot with cream on. How they love it? Weren't they glad?" said Katherine jokingly. "I heard how Emily brought a smile to your face each morning, but I am very short of milk this morning. I promise to do porridge tomorrow."

"That's okay, Mum, she did rather spoil me. But I am pleased my provision of a lunchtime snack on Saturday went down so well. You should have seen Emily's face, thinking she would have to survive on an ice-cream. Then when I said to look in my rucksack, she let out a squeak and positively beamed at me." He frowned slightly. "I keep feeling things are too good to be true, as if something terrible is about to happen."

"You can get thoughts of impending doom out of your head, son," his mother replied. "Remember the Gordons; they had 60 lovely years, and you chose exactly the right type of jewel for the ring yourself."

"Yes," said James, "but if it is a dream or a magic spell, she has put on me, I don't want to change a thing. After breakfast, I must be down the road to Orange Berries, so I can sweep up any litter that has blown into the car park. It was quite windy yesterday and particularly last night."

As James walked back along the drive he noted the trenches for the foundations of the extension. He realised they did not have any planning permission yet but hoped it would just be passed as a minor shed extension. *They can hardly stop you from digging a few holes on your own land,* he thought.

He arrived at the Orange Berries at 9:20am and set about cleaning up the outside. It was just as well, as rubbish had been blown hither and thither, but the athletic James soon had the place looking more inviting, even though Monday tended to be a quieter day.

One person who was feeling very down that morning was Aileen. She had not seen, never mind talked to anybody over the weekend, and this morning she was late for her bus to Wadesburgh. She had also caught a cold, and by the time she alighted and went into the firm of accountants she worked for, she was already coughing and sneezing.

She apologised for her lateness, but seeing how poorly she was, her employer suggested she was better off at home. The boss suggested it would be most helpful if she could do the rough cashbook for the few cheques that had arrived in the morning's post, then she could leave.

By 11:40am, feeling rather sorry for herself, Aileen was walking back down the Skye Road to her home. She realised she would either have to cook something for lunch herself, or walk back up the road to the Orange Berries Café, because her mother had gone to see a friend in Inverness and would not be back till late afternoon.

Having taken a couple of Paracetamol, she put on an old coat which was a bit warmer than the smart one she wore to work and changed her high heels for comfy walking shoes.

As she stepped out of her drive, a smart red car drew up and asked if she knew where the Orange Berries Café was.

"Yes," she answered and pointed back up the road towards town. "You went past it; it is about 400 yards along on the other side of the road."

"Thanks," said the driver, closing the window and zooming off before Aileen could say she was just going there herself and might have got a lift.

The car turned round a few yards along the road and sped past Aileen who tried to wave, but the driver was obviously not looking.

Aileen was almost in tears when she walked past the flash red Lexus in the car park and into the café. She hoped young James would be kind to her. But no, Mrs McCready came over to take her order, because James was tied up shifting goods that had just been delivered.

So, she sat and ate her cheese and tomato toastie with crisps and salad, brooding how everything had gone wrong — not just today, but over the last few weeks. James and Emily seemed to be all smiles and laughter anytime she saw them, and she had heard about the engagement, of course. *He should have chosen me*, she thought, *Emily gets everything*. The one thing that puzzled her was the naming of some seat made of rocks high up on the Great Glen Way. Again, it seemed to be something to do with Emily.

So, after lunch she thought she would get some fresh air and walk up the Great Glen Way to see what all the fuss was about. At least it was dry, even if a bit windy. What Aileen had not appreciated was how steep the Great Glen Way was after passing Rubha Ard, where she knew James lived.

By the time she got to the top and turned east along the path, she felt exhausted and quite hot. Nevertheless, she continued along until she spotted the sign to the seat. Now she was on the level — or at least minor inclines — there was a stiff breeze blowing, and she went from being very hot to quite cold. Even she began to realise this walk was perhaps not a good idea.

She continued to walk east, and then there it was — a very large stone seat. As she came up to the seat, she spotted something in a cavity underneath it. Peering down, realised it was a scarf in green tartan. *Probably belongs to James*, she thought, and quickly made use of it, wrapping it right round her neck. Then she turned and sat on the seat to take in the view over the loch.

She sat there for a few minutes, but then realised she was starting to shiver and better get home. Her cold was now making itself felt as again she started to cough and sneeze.

Standing up, still none the wiser as to why it was called Sant Columba's Seat, she set off back up the path. As she passed some very juicy looking blackberries, she leant over to pick some, but only succeeded in pricking her finger, drawing blood. She took a tissue from her pocket and wrapped it around her finger, then carried on walking.

As she turned the bend and looked onwards towards the Great Glen Way, who should be coming along, sketch pad in hand, but James.

Quite what came over Aileen at that moment even she would later say she did not know. But suddenly all her troubles seemed to stem from James and Emily, so she rushed up to James and started to punch and beat him on his chest.

Taken completely by surprise, James tried to push her away. "Stop it!"

But Aileen continued shouting and screaming at him, "You've ruined my life."

James, still puzzled to know what all this was about, said, "Aileen, please stop it." And this time he gave her a much harder push, so Aileen stumbled backwards.

Almost at the same time, James noticed she was wearing his scarf, so he took hold of one end. The effect of this was to temporarily strangle Aileen, but James immediately let go when he realised what was happening.

Aileen then grabbed James's sketch pad, opened it, smeared some blood from her finger, then closed it and hit poor James across his cheek with the pad.

Just then she spotted Mrs McCready coming along with her dog Rowan, who was barking at all the kerfuffle. Immediately Aileen rushed over to the woman, calling out as she passed, "You saw him. He tried to strangle me. I'll sue him for assault." Then she ran off down the path and was soon out of sight.

Both James and Mrs McCready temporarily stood as if some banshee had made its presence known and then disappeared as quickly as it had arrived.

"What was all the fuss about?" Mrs McCready asked. The dog had calmed down and stopped barking when he recognised the friendly James.

James replied," I don't know. She just rushed at me, wearing my scarf. I was not trying to strangle her. I just took hold of one end, just to check if it was mine. I often leave it up here as I am usually quite hot walking up the hill, but then take it off to cool down."

As no-one was hurt, they both decided to dismiss the matter, even though James's cheek smarted a bit.

"I think she might be developing a cold, as her voice was a bit strained," he suggested.

"Perhaps she has a high temperature. Things like that can affect people," said Mrs McCready.

As they parted, they agreed to keep the matter to themselves as nothing would be gained by upsetting Aileen.

Indeed, when James arrived home at about 5:45pm, he did not mention the episode to his mother, feeling that it would sound like telling tales out of school.

\*

When Aileen got home, she looked terrible and her mother, who had just got back, asked where had she been. Aileen, not really thinking straight, blurted out that James had tried to strangle her and that she had a nasty cold and had cut her finger.

Mrs Murphy immediately saw red. "I am not having my daughter treated like this, with no respect. I shall report this to the Police tomorrow."

In the meantime, Aileen collapsed on a chair. Her mother helped her take off her heavy winter coat and then made her a bowl of hot tomato soup. After that, she put her to bed with a cup of Lemsip.

The following day, Mrs Murphy rang the Police and was told to come to the office in Wadesburgh for Aileen to make a statement.

It was a few days later before Aileen was well enough to go to the police station, and by then she felt as though it had been a bit of a nasty dream and wanted to forget about it.

"He didn't really hurt me," she told her mother.

But while Aileen's feelings on the matter had subsided, Mrs Murphy was now enraged, as if half the Scottish nation was against her family. As a result, the story became rather embellished: It was James who had rushed up to Aileen, not the other way round; James had tugged at the scarf nearly strangling Aileen; even though it was a minor jolt, James had immediately let go as soon as he saw what was happening; as for the sketch pad, it was James who had hit Aileen across the head, several times — not the other way round.

On Saturday morning, a police officer called at Rubha Ard to get a statement from James.

Katherine was completely baffled and said she knew nothing of the matter. Not only that, she said she knew her gentle son would not dream of attacking anybody, never mind a girl. She told the officer that James was at work at the Orange Berries Café and would not be back till about 4:15pm, so he said he would call again later.

When James returned home from work just after 4pm, his mother immediately asked, "Have you seen Aileen lately?"

"Only on Monday afternoon, up near St Columba's Seat."

"Oh, what was she doing right up there?"

"Collecting blackberries, I think," James replied. "But she had cut her finger in the process. She was wearing my scarf, but I did not mind as it was a bit cold. In fact, I think she was going down with a cold, as her voice sounded a bit rough."

"Well, a police officer will be calling shortly to take a statement about an assault on Aileen," Katherine warned.

"What!" gasped James. "If anything, it was she who assaulted me. Mrs McCready was there, and we agreed to say nothing about it. It was as if Aileen had a funny five minutes."

At that moment there was knock on the door, and it was the policeman who had called earlier. James opened the door and showed him into the lounge.

"Can I get you a cup of tea?" he asked.

"That's very kind of you," the young officer said.

He then asked James a few questions about the incident, and then asked him to write down in his own words what had happened.

When all the official business was done, the officer told him, "I am not meant to offer an opinion, but this all seems to be a bit of a storm in a tea cup. I doubt you will hear anything further, as there does not seem to be enough evidence of an actual assault."

James said he was certainly not going to press any charges and volunteered that he had tried to be friends with Aileen, but she had always been a bit 'prickly'. He felt she acted as if the Orange Berries crew – the former school buddies who congregated in the café mostly on Saturday mornings – had some ulterior motive for trying to get her to join them.

The police officer took a mental note, rather than an official one, of what James said. Then he left, again repeating that he doubted they would hear anything more.

Indeed, they did not hear anything about it for over three weeks, during which time James noticed that Aileen did not make a single appearance at the café.

Instead, James and Emily were focused on having their plans drawn up for the joint workshop. These were then placed with the formal application documents and sent to the Highland Planning office by Emily's uncle.

Although they had yet to get approval, so in theory could be asked to knock down some of the walls now being erected by Emily's brother, the work nevertheless continued. Most was done on Sundays, with James acting as general labourer, mixing cement and shifting breeze blocks and stone. They progressed so well that it was not long before they were putting beams up for the roof. By luck, George had managed to find a pair of wooden garage doors being disposed of at a premises where he was working.

Finally, it was with great relief that the November meeting of the planning office approved their plans as a minor addition to an existing garage.

This allowed them to properly finish off the workshop, ready to accept a kiln when they had saved enough money to buy one.

\*

The shock came on the third week of November when James received an official letter, asking him to attend the Sheriff Court in Inverness, regarding an assault on Aileen Murphy. The date for the hearing was Monday, 27th November, 2023.

When he went to ask Mrs McCready to have the day off, she said she would have to close the café that day as she had been called as a witness to the event.

"I do not know what I am meant to tell anybody," she said, "but don't worry, James, as far as I am concerned you are the innocent party. I do, however, note that the Appellant is down as Mrs Siobhan Murphy, as though she is suing on behalf of her daughter. It seems to be a private prosecution."

When she was told, Emily was incensed that her beautiful, kind, gentle fiancé should be accused of assault. But she too thought it sounded like Mrs Murphy was pushing the matter rather than Aileen.

So, a week later, Emily drove Katherine, James, and Mrs McCready to the Sheriff Court in Inverness — or to give it its correct title, the court in the Sheriffdom of Grampian, Highland and Islands. The case would be called at 10am, so they made sure to be there by 9:30am.

The Justice of the Peace was a little late entering the court, having read all the various statements. The main delay was his suggestion that the case was so weak, and he asked Mrs Murphy if she wished to continue, bearing in mind all the expense that would arise.

However, Mrs Murphy insisted that the case be heard, as she privately felt she would look a bit silly stepping down at this stage.

So, the Justice of the Peace first heard from Aileen, but was slightly annoyed when all she said was "he might have hit me" and "he tugged on the scarf and strangled me". Aileen also admitted that the tug had only been "for a second", when of course James had realised what was happening and let go.

Mrs McCready was then called as a witness to the event, but she said she seemed to remember Aileen swiping James's face with his sketch pad rather than the other way round. She could not honestly say if James had pulled at the scarf and possibly strangled Aileen. However, she did say it seemed as if James was merely defending himself from Aileen, so might have pushed her away quite innocently.

The JP then called James, who backed up what Mrs McCready had said, namely that rather than assaulting Aileen he had been merely defending himself. He did add that Aileen had grabbed his sketch pad, smeared blood on some pages in the middle, then closed the book and hit him across the face.

The Justice of the Peace then withdrew for a short while, but asked to see the sketch pad and scarf. The key element was why James would smear blood across his work, and it was apparently Aileen's blood from a cut on her finger.

In short, it seemed it was just malicious prosecution. So, after only ten minutes, he returned to the court and said he was satisfied that no assault had taken place, pointing out that if James had hit Aileen there would not be blood on the inside pages of the sketch pad. He announced he was therefore fining Aileen £200. He also told Mrs Murphy that she should have listened to the court officials — and before that to her own solicitor — that there was not clear evidence of any assault on her daughter.

"While I am levelling a fine against Aileen of only £200, I am aware she may have herself been coerced into proceeding with this case." And he advised Mrs Murphy not to consider appealing, as almost certainly the Sheriff would come to the same conclusion and then the fine could be increased to several thousand pounds. With that, he left the court.

Outside the courtroom, James found Emily who promptly gave him a kiss. Looking across the foyer of the court, he saw the tearful Aileen and went over and put his hand on her shoulder.

"Aileen, we don't like having enemies in Inverbroch, so you must resolve to be my friend," he told her.

She could barely comprehend what James was saying and stammered quietly through her tears, "I am really sorry, James. I did not mean to hurt you. I don't know what came over me."

"I think we will just put it down as a bad hair day," said James.

Aileen gave a slight smile and was ready to turn away when Emily said in her Head Girl tone of voice, "No good turn goes unpunished, but equally, no bad turn goes unrewarded."

Aileen could not understand Emily's turn of phrase — one she used to baffle all the irate kids at school with.

"In short, my wee lassie, as you have been a wicked girl, we are all going across the road for a drink, and you are to join us as you will be paying the bill," Emily informed her. "However, you can deduct if from the £200 you owe James."

Aileen burst into tears again. "Why are you so kind to me?" she asked.

"Well, you go to church more often than we do," said James, "and what does the Lord's Prayer say? 'Forgive those who trespass against us.'"

Aileen gave a slight nod of recognition.

Aileen's mother, however, was nowhere to be seen. Undoubtedly annoyed at her daughter's performance, equally she could not deny that both Aileen and her solicitor had advised not to proceed, so all the expenses would be down to her.

James, Emily, Jane McCready, Katherine, and of course Aileen, decided not to go to a pub in Inverness, but go to the Fiddlers at Drumnadrochit. It was a pub Emily knew and one that would avoid the need to find a car park in town.

Aileen made a call to her mother on her mobile, but as it went straight to voicemail, she just said she had a lift home — not mentioning it was with the 'enemy'.

So, after about 45 minutes, they were parking in the car park just opposite Fiddlers, which was popular in the walking season with those doing the Great Glen Way, not to mention those thirsty after visiting the Loch Ness Centre.

Aileen was still feeling a bit unsure of herself and questioning whether the friendship offered by James, and particularly Emily, was genuine. As was already after 12:30pm, she offered to foot the bill for lunch.

"No," said Emily, "that is very kind of you, but we will all buy our own lunch. You just cover the drinks bill as agreed, otherwise your mother will be asking why you are suddenly bankrupt."

Aileen was quite pleased with that decision, as she was not due to be paid till the following week.

Lunch proved to be an entertaining event, as Jane McCready gave an account of some of the strange people that used to frequent the café some 20 years earlier — most of whom had since died. This included a Mr Terrence Thompsett, always known as Mr TT, who had the same thing every day — a tomato and cheese toastie with salad, followed by a toasted tea cake and a cup of Earl Grey tea. Then there was an old lady called Gladys, who lived in a tumbledown crofter's cottage along the Skye Road. She would only be there on Mondays, Wednesdays, and Fridays, would only eat half her lunch, and then tip the rest into a Tupperware box she brought with her. She had a ridiculously long tartan scarf, which she would wind round her neck, but then it often dragged on the floor in front of her. Amazingly, she never seemed to trip herself up or strangle herself.

At this point Aileen gasped, "Oh, James, did you get your scarf back?"

"Yes, thank you, both items. The scarf and sketch pad were passed to me as soon as we left the court."

After lunch they drove on to Inverbroch, dropping off Mrs McCready and Aileen, then returning to the Macdonalds' house, where Emily invited them in for a cup of tea. This allowed Katherine to update Emily's mother about the court case, while the two lovers escaped to Emily's bedroom, where the competition picture was still hanging.

The two of them stood for a moment looking at it until Emily broke the silence. "I note you always sign your work J Mackay not James!"

"I do it," said James very quietly, "as a tribute to my father, who always supported me. He was J Mackay as well, being John."

"Oh, that is lovely, James." She gave him a hug and a kiss. "You can have the painting back anytime you want it."

"No, I expect it to gather at least 60 years of dust before I take full possession of it."

Emily just smiled back, giving him a squeeze.

*Chapter 11*

# The Workshop Takes Shape

Over the following weeks, the workshop was gradually completed. The roof proved to be a bit tricky, particularly where the new part joined the original wooden building. But a lot of lead flashing ensured the damp did not get through. Soakaways were dug at some distance from the building to take the rain well away, and the concrete floor was extended to include the whole of the garage area. This avoided any step from garage to workshop, as well as making the whole floor area about four inches above the nominal ground level. This again would help to ensure that heavy rain flowed around rather than through the garage.

The interior of the workshop was then completed, including the plumbing, as George had already fitted the sewer pipe when doing the foundations and floor. And it only took an evening for Emily's father to fit the toilet with a small hand basin and a large Belfast sink with just a cold tap over it. The hand basin in the toilet had cold in-flow, but an electrical heater, which was fitted with infrared sensor, so water started to flow without actually having to touch anything. Obviously, the power input was yet to be fitted, but that would be done with the rest of the electrics.

It was now a question of having the electricity installed. They would need a 30amp socket to cope with the kiln, but also a few other 13amp sockets as well, plus suitable lighting.

James made a sketch of what was needed, adding distances along walls and ceiling heights, so they could gauge how much cable would be needed. Then he checked what the existing power cables rating was and went back to the house to determine where the supply came from. He was pleasantly surprised to find it was run off a 30amp fuse. It seemed the original occupants had probably used some power tools in the garage so had ensured they had adequate amperage available.

James then rang Robert down at Cut Lake, to see if he could help with the electrics. As it happened, he was still working on the house where Emily's father was doing the plumbing, so he popped by on a Friday evening to see what was involved. While there, he took James's sketch drawing so that he could provide a quote. With the job being in a workshop, he would not have to worry about wiring being channelled behind the plaster of walls, but could be put into trunking that could be stuck on walls and ceilings. He decided it should be a fairly easy job and would only take a couple of hours. He also confirmed that the existing power supply was adequate, which would save a lot of time and money.

It was agreed that he would do the work on Sunday, 10th December, with Katherine telling Robert to bring Ann and she would make lunch for them as a quid pro quo for them wining and dining James and Emily in the summer.

The previous week Emily had confided in Fiona that their joint workshop was just waiting on the electricity being installed, then all they would need was a workbench and a few shelves and they would be ready to go.

"What about the kiln?" asked Fiona. "Surely you need to put that in first?"

"Well," said Emily excitedly, "don't tell James yet, but it should be delivered this Wednesday. My dad has agreed to cover the bill for the kiln and the potter's wheel, and we can pay him back as soon as we can. I have managed to save about £2,000 already, and James's money will cover the building costs. So, when Robert comes up on Sunday — he's the guy whose wife owns 'the shed' — he will be able to put sockets exactly where they are needed. Then all we will need is a bench about 6 × 3 feet and a few shelves and we will be ready for business."

Fiona made a mental note about the bench and shelves, as she remembered there was a large solid table that was sitting at the back of Matthew's parents' garage. Later, she quietly had a word with her beau, who in turn found out that they just wanted to get rid of the table, as it was just getting in the way.

Sunday soon came, and Robert and Ann arrived at Rubha Ard just after 9am. Katherine invited Ann in for a chat and coffee, allowing Robert and James, acting as unpaid assistant, to get to work. Robert was impressed with the new shiny kiln and potter's wheel, and with the rating still stamped on the side of these new items he could ensure the appropriate power sockets were positioned and correctly fused. First, though, he installed a box with a number of circuit breakers, so that both new items could have their own breaker, and allowed the lights and remaining power sockets to have separate breakers.

James soon became quite skilled at cutting the lengths of trunking to put the cables in. This allowed Robert to deal with the connections from breaker to socket or light fitting. He had seen there would be a need for a couple of sets of spotlights — not just over the potter's wheel, but to light up a wall where the bench or James's easel would stand.

They took a brief break for coffee and biscuits at 11am, when Ann and Katherine came out to see how they were getting on. Then Emily arrived, carrying a basket with bottles of red and white wine, and she went in to help prepare the lunch for seven, as Emily's parents had been invited to the feast.

With just ten minutes before lunch was to be served up, Robert threw the switch in the house and checked everything was working in the workshop. The various lights all had pull switches since both painter and potter might have wet hands when they needed to turn lights on or off.

The lunch of roast chicken with all the trimmings was a great success. The two Roberts, of course, knew each other, but it was nice to chat and not feel guilty that they were neglecting their jobs of electrician or plumber.

At about 2:30pm, when the seven were enjoying a cup of coffee after lunch, they heard the sounds of someone playing a Scottish reel on a violin.

Unbeknown to the party inside, Matthew and a few of the Orange Berries crew had quietly unloaded the heavy old table off the roof of a car and managed to put up a couple of shelves. Then Fiona, with a flourish, produced a large white cloth, which was placed on the table with a dozen glasses, a couple of bottles of bubbly, and a large cake.

It was Fiona who began playing a reel on her violin, and the party inside came out to find out what was going on. They found that a long piece of red ribbon had been set across the double doors. And, with much clapping and cheering, Fiona invited James and Emily to declare their workshop open.

Smiling broadly, the pair accepted the scissors from Fiona and jointly cut the ribbon. When they opened the doors, they were surprised to see the table, which had been temporarily pressed into service to hold glasses and bottles of bubbly. Matthew duly opened some of the bottles and announced, "I declare these workshops open."

Once everybody had a glass of bubbly, to the surprise of everyone except James, Emily spoke up, "This seems a good time to announce we will be getting married on Saturday, 31st August, 2024, so put that date in your diaries.

"Unfortunately, we need to be quite selective as to who is invited to the wedding breakfast, because the hotel can only accommodate about 30 people. We are investigating options so that most people in the village can feel part of the celebrations, even if not actually be at the wedding breakfast. But everybody is invited to the kirk, which we hope to open just for the wedding service."

At that moment, who should walk up the drive but Aileen. She hesitated, unsure whether she might be intruding. However, James spotted her and said, "Aileen, you are just in time for a glass of bubbly."

"It's okay," Emily explained. "We are just celebrating the opening of our joint workshop."

Aileen then rather sheepishly took out a small parcel from a shopping bag she was carrying and said, "I bought this for you, James."

He was a little surprised to be receiving a present, but laughed when he saw it was a new scarf in Mackay tartan.

Aileen explained that she felt guilty about mucking up his old one, especially as it probably had blood on it.

"That is very kind of you," said James, and bent over and kissed her cheek.

Aileen paled a bit, and seeing she was a little embarrassed, James told her, "Put the 31st August, 2024, in your diary."

"Why?" asked Aileen, puzzled.

"Because you are invited to our wedding."

"Me?" squeaked Aileen in disbelief.

Emily came across to join them. "You have been rather kind to James, giving him a new scarf. But as no good turn goes unpunished, you are required to put on your best dress and be at the church at 12noon, then come to the meal at the Inverbroch Arms as penance."

Aileen smiled at Emily, still baffled by her back-to-front saying; secretly, she felt privileged to be asked.

*

For the next few days, not a lot happened in the workshop. Supplies of clay and glazes, and even a supply of mountboard, arrived to be duly stored, ready for when first James and then Emily would start to work there permanently.

It was fairly easy for James, as all he needed to do was to move his easel, paints, and brushes into the area earmarked for him, then slightly alter the direction of the overhead spotlights. The workshop had a large window at the rear, and although nearby shrubs tended to reduce the limited daylight, at least it was south-facing. Of course, lots of the great masters relied on a north-facing widow for light, as this tended to give a consistent light level. James, however, was not a portrait artist. So, for the various country views of lochs and mountains he could cope well enough.

Emily decided to keep working at the Clay Works at South Lewiston until March 2024, as she wanted to build up some reserve funds in her bank account and at least in part pay back some of the money her father had loaned her.

This did not mean the potter's wheel and kiln lay idle, though. Most Saturdays and Sunday mornings, she would be there working. She tended to produce a small number of items, perhaps four mugs and four plates on Saturday, then about 4pm she would be dipping them into her favoured glaze, carefully ensuring it had spread evenly over the pieces, then load them into the kiln. The timer was set to turn off after about 10 hours, but it took a few trials to be sure appropriate temperatures had been reached. For glazed items, this was 1257C; where the clay items were heated without a glaze, it only needed to reach 1,000C. Emily knew what to expect, having gone through the process dozens of times on her course at Edinburgh, and gaining further experience by working at South Lewiston.

Over the months she started to build up quite a collection of saleable items and many were now displayed in the craft shop. Only a few sold in October and November, but there was a marked pick-up in sales as Christmas approached.

At the beginning of December, Emily realised that James would be twenty shortly before Christmas and was mindful that a party should be organised. However, she decided to tell James that she was thinking of arranging a pre-Christmas party, without mentioning a date. To throw him off the scent, she said that it had been Fiona's idea and it was to be before Christmas, as she knew lots of people would be away from town staying with relatives over the festive period.

The question was where to hold it. One idea that Fiona came up with was in the Orange Berries Café. She suggested that a lot of the girls and even some of the boys would be happy to come with suitable dishes of salad or sausage rolls, or even chicken legs. One young lad said he was sure he could get his father to get their pizza oven running that day and deliver maybe half a dozen freshly cooked pizzas.

So, one Saturday when James was in the café kitchen doing the last of the day's washing up — most of which went in the dishwasher — Emily went in to help him, allowing Fiona to approach Mrs McCready for permission to use the cafe. She was happy to agree so long as the place was ready for business by Monday morning — even if they did the clearing up on the Sunday.

The date for the actual party was decided as Saturday, 16th December — three days before James's birthday.

In the end, rather than try and find some suitable present relating to an artist, Emily bought him a rather smart colourful shirt. However, to the Orange Berries crew, if they wanted to club together, Emily suggested he could do with a better easel to replace the rather dilapidated one he was using at the moment.

\*

On the Saturday of the surprise party, as soon as business was finished for the day, Emily walked with James to Rubha Ard so that Fiona and her helpers could quickly set up the café.

Having arrived at the house, Emily told him, "I am not sure I will be around on your birthday on Tuesday. There is some kind of production meeting at the clay works about next year, so I had better be there. Would you like to take this and try it on now?"

James was a little puzzled, as well as disappointed that his bonnie lass would not be around for a birthday drink. Nevertheless, he opened the present, which Emily had been hiding, and he was impressed with the choice of colours. Emily, of course, had an eye for these sorts of things. So, with a smile, he put it on and gave her a thank you kiss.

His mother then called out that she had made them a cup of tea and a plate of goodies for them to take to the Christmas party that night.

James tripped down stairs and thanked his mother. "I had forgotten all about that. Emily, when are we due there?"

"Don't you worry, my wee laddie, it does not start until six o'clock, so we have plenty of time."

Emily turned the conversation to planning their wedding. "It would be nice to use the church here in Inverbroch, but Pat the Pier MacDonald — no relation, I might add— can tell you who the last minister was, but just says it was being sold as a private house. I've sent emails to various people to find out who now owns it, but so far, no joy. I am hoping the Scottish Land Registry will come up with an answer, but it will be at least a week before I hear anything."

"I wonder if the Inverbroch Arms has been registered as a place you can hold a wedding," said James. "Although in such circumstances you cannot have any Bible readings or hymns."

Emily looked thoughtful. "Well, perhaps we should be off to the church at Drumnadrochit this Sunday and ask the vicar there how things might work."

There was much pondering about where to hold the wedding service, and if it might be Drumnadrochit they would need to have the service quite early — at 11am — to give time for the service and return to Inverbroch. This discussion went on so long that it had gone six o'clock before they realised the time.

James, looking smart in his birthday shirt, took Emily's hand and announced, "Miss Emily, would you like to escort me to a party tonight? It is being held at the Orange Berries Café. I think you may know some of the people that will be there, but don't worry, I'll look after you."

"*Touché*," said Emily, and they both burst into laughter. "That would be very kind of you, good sir. Will there be any dancing?"

"We might manage to strip a willow or two, or even follow that with the Dashing White Sergeant," replied James.

So, carrying plates of sausage rolls and samosas, they tripped down to the café. When they arrived, there was hardly a light on and everything was quiet.

But when they opened the door, a great chorus of Happy Birthday rang out, with Fiona playing the tune on her violin.

Initially, James was trying to determine whose birthday it was until his eyes rested on a banner saying: *JAMES Happy 20th Birthday.*

"But it's on Tuesday," he said, turning to Emily.

"We know," she smiled, giving him a hug. "But most of us will be at work, so we hope you don't mind celebrating a little early."

At that point James was showered with lots of birthday cards and even a few small presents.

With a big smile on his face, he thanked everybody, adding, "I get the feeling the wicked witch form the north had a hand in all this," to which there was a lot of laughter.

Drinks were handed out, with most taking a glass of a specially prepared fruit punch as the cafe did not have an alcohol license.

An area had been cleared so there could be some dancing. Andrew Rogers, a young lad who was a friend of Fiona, had brought along his keyboard, so with Fiona on violin they struck up a suitable tune for The Dashing White Sergeant. Most people knew the moves, so with sets of 6, 3 opposite 3, they took to the floor. Some threes had to be made of 3 boys, but it did not matter. They then decided on the Gay Gordons, where of course James immediately grabbed Emily's hand.

"That reminds me," said Emily, "we had better let the Gordons know the date of the wedding, as it would be nice to invite them."

After this dance, most people collapsed and felt it was time to attack the food. So many different dishes had been brought to the party feast that Fiona was urging people not to be frightened about heaping up their plates, as it would only go to waste.

Andrew then gave an impromptu performance, playing tunes from shows, where many knew the words. The need for extra lubrication to sing soon emptied the punch bowl, which was just as well. This meant the remaining fruit could be put into small bowls, with an accompaniment of a scoop of ice cream being offered to any takers.

It was about 9:30pm when Emily, in her best Head Girl voice, suggested it was time to draw matters to a close. They decided to wash up all the plates, glasses, bowls, and cutlery that evening, although a lot went into the dishwasher. But they left sweeping the floor and replacing tables and chairs where they should be until the next day.

Emily explained that she would not be around until the afternoon, as she and James needed to go to the church at Drumnadrochit in the morning. So, everyone agreed to meet about 2:30pm.

When James walked Emily back to her house, she gave him a goodnight kiss before owning up.

"Don't worry, I lied about Tuesday. I will be around in the evening. I just wanted to make sure you were appropriately dressed for the occasion tonight."

"Oh, being wicked again?" laughed James. "No good turn goes unpunished, so on Tuesday you had better meet me at the Inverbroch Arms, and you can buy the drinks."

"Of course," said Emily. "Why don't you ask your mother to come along, and I'll ask my parents? I always feel guilty leaving your mother all on her own."

"That is a very kind idea," James replied. "We can meet there on the Tuesday at 8 o'clock."

With that, James gave Emily one more kiss and was off on his way back to Rubha Ard.

## Chapter 12

# The Wedding is Planned

Tuesday evening came, and Emily was as good as her word, buying their group drinks that evening at the Inverbroch Arms. Of course, the conversation soon turned to the coming nuptials.

Katherine offered to contribute to the cost. "Weddings cost an awful lot these days. My parents got away with a few drinks and sandwiches, and there was no sit-down meal as such. Nowadays, guests expect not only a two or three course meal, but a band with dancing as well."

Emily chipped in that she hoped to repay most of the kiln and wheel costs by March, using her earnings from the Clay Works, but said she would have to hold back about £1,500 to buy a small second-hand van. She was starting to get a few orders from far and wide, and posting such items was quite difficult, not just in the packing but the cost of delivery.

Christmas was quiet. James invited Emily over on Boxing Day and very sensibly they spent the time deciding how they might improve their finances. They took a number of digital pictures of some recent and some older pictures James had painted, managing to put together a set of Winter, Spring, Summer, and Autumn, as well as several others.

They then invested a few hundred pounds and carefully used an online printing company that specialised in producing greetings cards. They left the inside blank, so the card could be used for any occasion. It was apparent from the costing that by buying a block of 100 cards, with the discount of 15%, they could reduce the cost of a saleable card with an envelope in a cellophane sleeve to just 47p each. They also found if they spent more than £500, they got the postage free.

Their efforts took all afternoon, so it was 5:30pm when Katherine shouted upstairs, "Would you two lovers like to come down for a spot of tea?"

They shouted back, "Yes please."

Emily leant over and gave James a kiss. "Well, we are lovers now," she said with a big grin on her face.

Katherine was intrigued with their money-spinning exercise and said she would definitely be buying a few cards. She often found she needed a card, and even though she worked at the shop from time to time, inevitably she would forget to buy one until she got home.

*

Emily and James, and their parents, attended the Hogmanay celebrations held at the community hall, where they welcomed the new year in with thoughts of the coming wedding.

After the celebrations were over, everything returned to normal. James was back selecting sketches that he considered worth converting to paintings, to build up a choice of pictures for display at the craft shop. Pictures were now framed and priced at £200 or more, depending on size.

At the end of January, Emily decided to look out for a suitable small van. But it soon became obvious that she would need to be spending at least £4,500 to find anything decent, and even then it was likely to be over six years old. Then, quite by chance, she found they could hire an almost new van for about £200 a month. Even with added insurance costs, this looked like a better option.

So, early in February, Emily got a small Citroen Berlingo on hire from a dealer in Inverness. They even delivered it, for no extra cost. The fact that it had three seats in front was very helpful, as it meant Emily could not only take James, but also Katherine if they wanted to do some shopping in Inverness. As she now drove it to work at South Lewiston, it also meant her mother could have her car back, to go to yoga classes in Fort William.

The next important task was to produce a wedding invitation. Lots of people would be booking summer holidays, so the sooner they officially knew the date, the better. The one thing they had failed to do was to be able to use the old church, so in the end they decided on the church at Drumnadrochit.

They spent most of a Sunday afternoon quietly producing the invitation, with some discussion on whether to use both Emily's Christian names because James had only one. In the end, they agreed on both for Emily, and they were pleased with the final design.

---

Mr Robert & Mrs Margaret Macdonald
and Mrs Katherine Mackay
request the pleasure of your company
at the marriage of their children,
Emily Margaret to James,
on Saturday, 31st August, 2024 at 11am
at the Parish Church of Urquhart & Glenmoriston
Kilmore Road, Drumnadrochit, IV63 6UG

and afterwards at Inverbroch Arms Hotel at 1pm
RSVP Macdonald Towers, Inverbroch, or by email
margaret@macdonaldtowers.co.uk

---

Finally happy with their efforts, they went downstairs to get Katherine's approval.

"Yes, that's fine," she said. "It does not need to be too elaborate, just state the essentials, which all seem to be there. I like the green edging, and it is a nice touch to put the picture of the church in it."

The only part of the celebrations not mentioned was the ceilidh in the evening, which Emily and James were paying for and decided to keep to themselves. Before they came downstairs, Emily said secretly to James that she would be making a short speech after they had eaten their wedding meal and would announce the ceilidh then.

The previous Sunday they had met the Reverend Dr Benjamine Becula, who was the acting minister for the enlarged parish of Urquhart & Glenmoriston. They had also attended an odd service or two — either at the Old Farm on the lochside, which was further down from where Emily lived, or at the community hall. For lochside services, they discovered they needed to bring a chair or be standing though the whole service.

*

On Saturday, 17th February, 2024, James suggested that they deliver a wedding invitation to the Gordons. They knew it was a bit of a gamble, as they might already have something arranged — particularly as it was so close to the Gordons' wedding anniversary date. Nevertheless, just after lunch, they set off on the 80-plus miles round trip.

Emily was being good and not making silly jokes and losing her concentration. This was just as well, as twice she got cut up by a couple of speeding driver who were probably racing each other, even overtaking her as they approached a bend. James and Emily exchanged smiles when 20 minutes later they passed the two cars stopped at the side of the road by a police car.

"Driving without due care and attention," said Emily with a smile on her face.

As they passed, James noted the drivers were being breathalysed, and he quietly giggled to himself.

"I am not sure that is very friendly," commented Emily.

"Well, I was thinking about you and have come up with a silly ditty.

> While driving along the Great Scottish Glen
> She's much more careful than most of the men.
> For our Milly Molly Mandy only drinks shandy
> And would turn down anybody who offers her brandy."

Emily laughed. "Well, my wee laddie, if you are going to learn to drive, I expect you to be teetotal as well."

"Don't worry," replied James, "all my earnings are going into my savings account."

Shortly afterwards they spied the sign for Glen Finnan. "We need to take a right at the roundabout, then we follow the railway. Then after Corpach, it is the second station we need."

Although not driving very fast, they passed two houses just before Locheilside Station. So, they turned round at the station, which was easy as no other cars were parked there. Then carefully drove back, turning into the drive for Station House.

They bravely walked up to and knocked on the front door, which was on the railway side, rather than the main road side. The door was opened by Charlotte, who was all smiles when she saw who it was.

"Oh, do come in, how wonderful to see you. How are you two getting on? I think a workshop was in the offing when we met last year." Then before either Emily or James could answer, she asked, "When are you two getting married?"

"Oh," said Emily, "that's what we came to tell you." She handed Charlotte the invitation. "The wedding is on Saturday, 31st August this year, and it would be lovely if you could be there. With our engagement rings matching, I rather look on you as a fairy godmother. Although," she laughed, "I am often called the wicked witch from the north, so there could be a clash of wands."

As all three burst into laughter, Calum appeared to see who had arrived.

"Oh, how nice to see you again," he said. "Do go into the lounge and I'll put the kettle on. We were about to have a cup of tea, and I think there are some chocolate biscuits somewhere."

They moved into a large room with two long settees, making themselves comfortable on one which had a rather lovely view across Loch Eil.

Charlotte looked closely at the invitation. "This is nice of you to invite us. Are you sure you want two old fogies like us there? And the date looks okay, even though the Saturday is actually our anniversary. It was a Saturday 61 years ago, but this year I think things will be a bit quieter. We might manage a slow waltz, but I think the Dashing White Sergeant may be a bit too much for us."

"Well," said Emily, "I suppose we could have the Gay Gordons in your honour."

James interjected, "You can see why Emily is called the wicked witch."

At that point there was more laughter.

Calum came in with a tray bearing cups, a large teapot, and of course the chocolate biscuits.

James continued, "She had me doing the Gay Gordons when we first met, and she has had me under a spell ever since."

"I don't think you've ever complained, my wee county man," Emily laughed.

Puzzled, Calum asked what she meant by 'county man'.

"Oh, that is from when I was at school," explained James. "There was a lot in the newspapers about the county signs for Mackay County in north Sutherland being vandalised, and someone in my class said, 'Here comes the County Man.' The nickname stuck. I don't mind, though, as very few people round here have the surname Mackay. I get my own back by calling Emily the wicked witch from the north."

"Well," said Charlotte, "I think I had better live up to my chosen persona as fairy godmother and be there to ensure everything goes according to plan. I am sure it will."

They sat sipping their tea, thinking how peaceful it all was with the view across the loch and the mountains beyond. James was tempted to ask if he could make a quick sketch, but before he could excuse himself to get his pad from the car, a steam train passed, slowing down as it was approaching the station only about 200 yards ahead.

"Your grandchildren must love coming here to visit you," commented Emily.

"Oh yes," said Calum, "there have been many pictures of steam trains drawn by the children; indeed, you can see the gradual improvement of scale and perspective as they grow older. Our Finlay — like you, James — has developed a natural eye for landscape painting, and we have many of his pictures of the view across the loch."

James decided not to get his sketch pad as he didn't want to tread on their grandchildren's toes by emulating views across the loch.

Emily produced a small gift of two small plates with her trademark blue and green lines, reflecting the Mackay tartan colours. She handed them to Charlotte wrapped up in tissue paper.

"From my latest batch," she said.

Charlotte took them, and on removing the tissue-paper said, "Oh how lovely. That is kind of you. How is the pottery business going?"

"It was a bit slow at first," admitted Emily, "but I am starting to get a few orders, and with deliveries and the need to collect things like clay and glazes, you will see we have hired a van. Turns out it was cheaper to hire one than buy one, and this one is less than a year old. There is a possibility of a big order coming from the hotel where the wedding breakfast will be held. Fingers crossed!"

"Well, I am pleased you are doing well, I suppose if we see some more plates like these at the wedding, we will know you have hit the jackpot."

"Yes," replied Emily. "At the moment I am only producing my own wares on Saturdays and Sundays. During the week I am up at the Clay Works at South Lewiston, as that way, I am definitely going to have some money coming in at the end of each month. I still owe my father quite a bit, as he stumped up for the cost of the kiln and potter's wheel."

Looking out across the loch, James said, "Shadows are appearing, so I think we had better be off."

Emily looked up and acknowledged his comment. "Yes, I am not too keen on driving in the dark. What's the time now?"

"Just after four o'clock," said Calum, pointing to a clock on a sideboard at the end of the room.

"Right, that should be okay. It takes us about an hour and 20 minutes and it will be dark about 5:30pm, so we should be home by then."

Charlotte showed them out, saying how lovely it had been to see them again. She said she was pleased that all was going well and was already looking forward to their big day.

Emily was careful as she emerged from the Gordons' drive, as it was slightly uphill. As they journeyed home, they said very little. But after they passed the turning to 'the shed', Emily said, "I am really pleased we have invited them. They were obviously pleased to see us. I must make a mental note to remember that the day of our wedding will be their sixty-first anniversary."

Then, with a tear in her eye, she said, "They are like a good luck charm. I wonder what Calum did before he retired. He seemed to appreciate his grandchildren's efforts at drawing and painting."

"I think he may have been an architect," James replied. "There was some sort of certificate from the Royal Institute of British Architects on the wall near the front door.

As they were nearing home, Emily said, "My mother has tea ready for us at six. Don't worry, I warned your mother not to expect us back for tea. She is always getting us tea, so it is about time she had a day off."

A few minutes later they pulled up to 'Macdonald Towers', which was now the semi-official name of Emily's home. To their surprise, Katherine was already there, with both mothers keen to know how they had got on.

"Wonderfully," said Emily. "The Gordons were really pleased to see us, and believe it or not, our wedding day is actually the same day as their sixty-first, yet they still want to come."

With all the excitement and the long journey home, the two lovers were delighted to tuck into a bowl of Cullen Skink and some ham sandwiches, not to mention chocolate cake with a dollop of ice cream.

*

Over the next few days, they made up a definitive list of who would be at the sit-down meal at the hotel. It helped that they now knew to reserve two places for the Gordons.

Emily had already sounded out Fiona and Yvonne about being her bridesmaids, and they both jumped at the request.

James, meanwhile, was wondering to who to ask to be his best man.

"Why don't you ask your cousin Allan," suggested his mum. "It would only be three people on your limited list of 30, as Allan's parents would obviously expect to be there. Allan's sister is in New Zealand, so it would be a rather expensive exercise for her and her husband to come."

The next day James rang his cousin, who still lived in Tongue in Mackay County. Allan was delighted to be asked, and the pair enjoyed a long chat in which James told him all about his beautiful Emily and why she was known as the wicked witch.

"Don't worry, though," he assured Allan, "her teasing and tricks are never malicious. When she was Head Girl, she used to defuse any conflict with one of her peculiar sayings — particularly 'No good turn goes unpunished', which so flummoxed the warring parties that they always stopped fighting and wandered off asking each other what she meant."

Allan confided that he had broken up with his long-term girlfriend Carol a couple of months ago. James could see an interesting possibility emerging and, putting on Emily's witch's hat, said, "You will remember that I am known as the county man, so now there will be two county men. And I know one of the girls we have invited will be intrigued by that."

"What is she like?" asked Allan, aware his cousin was match-making.

James simply replied, "Oh, she is quite attractive, but of Irish descent. However, I think perhaps you will be concentrating on your accountancy exams for now, so you'll have to wait and see." He finished the call by saying, "I'll put an official invite for you and your parents in the post."

He went into the kitchen to update his mother, saying Allan was really pleased to be asked, especially as it would be after his final accountancy exams in June.

"Well," said his mother, "I must send him a good luck card for the exams. As soon as you get your greeting cards, I'll send one off."

*

Over the next few months, they kept thinking of things that needed to be done, particularly on the big day. Should they have some flowers for the church? Should there be little posies on the tables at the Inverbroch Arms? The latter could be sorted by asking the hotel what could be done and if they knew anyone who could help. It turned out they were most obliging and got the florist, Linda Kelsey, to ring James.

A few days later she came out to meet them at the Macdonalds' house, where she showed them photos of what could be provided. They quickly agreed on the small vases of flowers for each table at the hotel, but they were a little concerned about having flowers in the church for just an hour or so, and then they would go to waste.

Linda said, "Oh no, they come in self-standing or hanging wire baskets, so you or your ushers can take them away immediately afterwards."

Delighted they could be used again, Emily said, "Brilliant, they could come back here and brighten up the village hall for the ceilidh."

Linda asked what she wanted to do about the bridal bouquet and possibly some for the bridesmaids."

"I think we will just have a bouquet for me," Emily replied, "as we have a limited budget."

Over the following weeks, other questions popped up, like who should be ushers. So, a quiet word was had with Matthew and Yvonne's boyfriend William. And Emily said she would ask her brother to be Chief Usher, being a little older. She also wanted him to drive his truck to the wedding so he could arrange gathering up the flowers and getting them to the village hall after the ceremony.

Although Emily had originally said she would stop work at the Clay Works at the end of March, she decided to stay on until the end of June. That way they would have extra funds to cover the village hall hire costs. They also needed someone to run a bar at the hall. So, they asked the hotel if they could accommodate them, which they were happy to do.

Although there would be a basic cost, which would include the first drink, after that people would have to stump up if they wanted to continue drinking. They hoped that would also stop people drinking too much.

Originally James and Emily had kept the ceilidh a secret, but it soon became clear they would have to own up. They could hardly go round the village saying to everybody they met to come to their wedding ceilidh, yet somehow keep it a secret.

They decided to tell their parents what they had planned, but to emphasised that they would cover the cost themselves. They all thought it was a lovely idea to be able to allow everyone to be involved and be part of the celebrations.

Briefly Emily wondered if they should have a Greek theme to the evening and hope everybody would pin money on her dress, which would offset their own outlay. But on further thought, she realised that wasn't really practical at a Scottish ceilidh.

The other issue that became evident was that guests would be wanting a bite to eat at about 7pm, particularly those who had not been at the wedding meal.

But Katherine was quick to solve the problem. "Don't worry, I'll get the village baking group to provide some goodies as they did at the ceilidh last August."

*

One Tuesday morning in late April, Emily was lying in bed thinking about what else needed to be organised, when she suddenly jumped up.

"My wedding dress!" she shouted.

Quickly dressing, she rushed down to the kitchen. "Mum, I have forgotten all about my wedding dress."

Her mother burst out laughing. "Oh Milly, calm down. I have already arranged to go into Inverness with Yvonne and Fiona this Saturday, but I was wondering how long it was going to take you before you realised you would be walking up the aisle in just your undies. If you had not thought of it by this Thursday, I was going to remind you."

She gave her daughter a hug. "I am glad you are human and forget the obvious now and again. You seem to have remembered everything else. Have you decided if your bridesmaids are wearing white as well? I have warned Charlotte Smith Bridal Boutique to expect us about 10am, so I have said to Fiona and Yvonne to be here at 9am."

"Oh, thanks, Mum," said Emily, breathing a sigh of relief that her mother had everything arranged.

On Saturday the group arrived at the boutique just before ten and were met by an elderly lady called Janice, who was most helpful. Emily plumped for a simple gown which finished just above the ground, with no train so that she could easily dance in it. The bridesmaid dresses were to be a very smart burgundy colour, and when they all stood together, they looked really lovely.

To Emily's delight, her mother said she would foot the bill for the dresses. "After all," she explained, "when your brother eventually makes an honest woman by proposing to Felicity, I will not have to fork out for that wedding dress."

The outfits would need a few slight adjustments, particularly for Emily. As she was quite tall, the hem would need to be let down by just under one inch, and the bodice would need to be loosened to accommodate her ample bosom. The boutique would email them when they were ready for a final fitting, and if everything was fine they could take the dresses away then.

By a little after 11:30am, they were on the way home. Emily was relaxing in the front seat, happy that all the important things were now in place, when she suddenly sat bolt upright and said rather loudly, "Shoes."

Emily's mother, who was driving, scolded, "Emily, for goodness' sake, calm down. The dress is so long you could be barefoot, or if it is raining you could wear your wellies."

Fiona and Yvonne, sitting in the back, started to laugh. "Yes, let's all wear Wellingtons," said Yvonne.

Emily turned and frowned. "Don't be rotten."

"You're not the only person that can be wicked," giggled Fiona.

Emily relaxed again, realising any smart shoe would do. Then, smiling, she added, "I think James would like me to wear my glass slippers!"

They drove on in almost silence, but as they were turning at the junction in Drumnadrochit, Emily again shouted out. "The minister!"

Her mother was quite cross this time. "Milly, what has got into you? You're normally cool, calm, and collected."

"Sorry, Mum, but as we are here, we could deliver an invitation to him and his wife and save postage." So, they drove round to the church and left an envelope for the Reverend Dr Benjamine Becula & Mrs Becula.

Almost home, Fiona suggested, "I think rather than a hen night, we had better have a spa weekend to calm you down before the big day. To recharge your batteries, so to speak."

Emily laughed, "I'll need to have recharged my wand by then as well."

*

One Saturday in early June, Katherine came out while both Emily and James were busy working in their new workshop, bringing them a cup of coffee and some biscuits.

"Why don't you come to Sunday lunch here tomorrow?" she asked Emily. "I have a proposition to put to you both."

"That sounds intriguing," replied Emily with a smile on her face.

Katherine just said, "I'll have lunch ready for about one o'clock, but don't worry, I am sure you will be pleased with what I am proposing."

Emily wanted to know more but bit her tongue. *While our parents have to trust us, I had better get used to trusting my mother-in-law-to-be,* she thought to herself. Out loud, she replied that she would organise her work so she could break off at the agreed time.

The next day Emily was at her pottery workshop early, loading up the latest batch of plates and mugs she had produced, carefully dipping them into freshly prepare glazes. By the time Katherine arrived with a morning coffee for the two artisans, Emily was ready to throw the switch and turn on her kiln.

This allowed her a couple of hours to tidy up — something she kept saying she must do but often ended up putting off!

With everything looking neat by ten to one, she was ready to move into the house to have this mysterious lunch. As the two lovers entered Rubha Ard they were both surprised to find Emily's parents already there, having slipped passed unnoticed.

Katherine told them go into the dining room with the instruction, "We're having basil and tomato soup first, and no questions until we have finished our starters."

Instead, Emily's father asked James, "How are you getting on? Have you sold any more pictures at the gallery at Fort William."

James replied, "I have just sold two small scenes of Eileen Doonan Castle, which is apparently a popular subject — so much so that the gallery owner said he would welcome a couple more and is sure he can sell them quickly. I suppose gallery owners keep a watchful eye on what types of scenes sell fast; after all, they have bills to pay like the rest of us."

Once they all finished their soup, Emily dutifully took the bowls to the kitchen, then she helped bring out some of the dishes for the main course — poached salmon, plus new potatoes, haricot beans, and carrots.

When everybody had been served, Katherine broke the tension that she detected on the faces of Emily and James. "Have you given thought to where you might live once you are married?"

Emily replied, "We have been a bit distracted by trying to get both businesses running smoothly. However, we were thinking we might rent somewhere locally; so far, though, nowhere seems to be appropriate. They are either so rundown that you feel they would need to be decontaminated before you moved in, or so expensive you would need to raise a mortgage to pay the rent, which of course is ridiculous."

"Well," said Katherine, "I have already discussed this with your parents, and the answer is rather staring us in the face. Or to put it bluntly, above us as we sit here. Upstairs there are four bedrooms and four en-suite bathrooms, because this place used to be run as a B&B. So, if you two were at the west end and I stay where I am in the east end, how would that suit you? And before you worry about any noise you might make playing the latest pop record or whatever, there would be at least a fire door between us."

Initially there was silence as the two would-be lodgers thought about being able to share a bedroom —maybe even before they got married.

As this point Robert broke the silence. "We realise it is no good us parents pretending that you two have been happy to be celibate and wait until the big day. After all, there are couples up and down the country sleeping together who are not even engaged and not thinking of getting married yet often have several children. And if Emily moved in here, it would help us when we have friends staying." He added mischievously, "I am sure you two will be happy to share James's double bed."

Emily and James were a little embarrassed, although delighted with the idea, so they still kept silent.

Katherine offered, "I must say I would be delighted if you did come and live here, Emily. If you both were away somewhere else, I would be rattling round this great big house and be down at the Orange Berries every day just so I could talk to somebody."

James and Emily looked at each other and smiled.

"Well," he said to her, "I think the high priestess has made you an offer you can't refuse!"

Emily nodded. "If you put it like that, when can I move in?"

With that the whole party started laughing.

"Tonight, if you like," said Katherine, noticing how Emily was looking longingly at her beau.

"Really?" gasped Emily. "Em, well, would Monday be okay, as that would give me an opportunity to at least get some clothes and essential items over here?"

"Monday it is," replied Katherine. "Obviously I am used to cooking for myself and James, but one extra mouth to feed will not be a problem."

"Oh, you must let me do some of the cooking, and I will do my share of the housekeeping, such as laundry," said Emily.

So, on Monday evening at about 7pm, Emily arrived with several cases full of clothes, as well as personal items. Katherine had been warned her future daughter-in-law might be a little late for dinner while she collected her initial batch of clothes from her parents' house. Emily had spent Sunday evening packing so that she could pick up the cases when she returned from work.

Later that evening, it was no surprise to Katherine that the two were saying they were ready for bed by 9:30pm.

*

The months of summer went by quickly, and Emily managed to produce a substantial number of plates cups and saucers, as well as some bowls in her signature design, with its navy blue and dark green rings round the edge of each item. She was hoping the hotel would decide on revamping their chinaware, but in the busy holiday season they had their mind on other things.

The last but one weekend of August approached, and Fiona had made all the arrangements for a day away in lieu of a hen party. This was for a dozen of the girls who knew and were friends with the former Head Girl, including Felicity, Emily's brother's girlfriend. The cost of two nights at a spa hotel had proved simply too expensive, so instead Fiona had arranged for an all-day pampering session, including a massage and use of the swimming pool. They even stayed for an early evening meal, which meant they were off home by 9pm, with the drivers all being very good and not drinking any alcohol.

# Chapter 13

# Oh Yes, I Will

On the Thursday evening before the big day, James and Emily sat down at Rubha Ard to check that they had everything organised, including confirming that all the invited guests had responded and were coming. For most, this was the wedding of the year and something they were definitely not going to miss. Everyone had confirmed their attendance, so the couple rang the hotel to confirm the number was indeed 30, with a top table for 12.

James reported that he had carried out his duties and had arranged for a plush white Rolls Royce wedding car to take Emily and her father, plus the bridesmaids, to the church. Emily would, of course, be temporarily back staying at Macdonald Towers, where her wedding dress and those of the bridesmaids had been carefully stored.

"They should be ready by 10:35am, as the journey time is in theory 19 minutes. That means you have six minutes spare, or 11 if you feel you need to exercise your right to be a little late," joked James.

Emily just smiled at this last remark. "Don't worry, my mother is all geared up to pick up Fiona and Yvonne at about 8:30am, so they will have time to put on their dresses. And a hairdresser friend of Yvonne's will be there to ensure we are all neat and tidy. My mother is driving herself to the church, because it will just be you and me coming back in the Rolls."

She sighed before continuing, "I have waited a year for this moment, and I don't intend to wait any longer than necessary. So, you had better be there when I arrive, or your dream may come to a crashing end."

"Well, we better not let that happen, my wicked witch," laughed James. "After all, there would be a lot of other disappointed people if your spell was broken."

"It's okay, my bonnie lad, my wand has been fully charged." With that she gave him a loving kiss.

As a basic check, they talked through the day and could not find anything they had forgotten. So, shortly before 9 o'clock James gave his beautiful bride a kiss, and she left to return to her family home. And they did not meet on the Friday evening, as that could invite bad luck.

Saturday came, and amazingly it was dry, reasonably warm, and sunny. Naturally, everyone in both the Mackay and Macdonald households was up early and slightly on tenterhooks with the impending nuptials.

Allan and his parents were staying at Rubha Ard, and he would be driving them, along with Katherine and James, to the church at about at 10:15am.

In the end, they arrived at the church a good 20 minutes early, where they were a little surprised to find a host of James and Emily's school pals already there.

Fiona had come up with the idea, which she had delegated to Matthew, for a dozen of the couple's former school pals to each hold up a large sunflower or blue hydrangea, with a background of a few branches from their own gardens, forming a floral passageway into the church.

And inside, the florist Linda Kelsey had done a wonderful job, as the church was suitably decorated with posies of flowers hanging at the end of each pew, as well as a stunning set piece on the altar. She had arranged for a friend who lived at

Inverbroch to deliver the bride's bouquet to the Macdonalds residence separately that morning.

At 10:20am the Rolls Royce arrived at the Macdonalds' house, and the bride, her father, and the two bridesmaids took their seats for the journey to Drumnadrochit. Perfectly on time, the Rolls Royce glided up Kilmore Road to stop opposite the path to the church where they were met by a magical scene, as the floral guard of honour stood to welcome them. They stepped into the church at precisely 11 o'clock, tears already in Emily's eyes as they passed through the magical floral entrance.

As she came up to the altar, James stepped forward to take the hand of his wonderful bride. He had thought of joking, "Do you come here often?" But he was worried that Emily might get a fit of the giggles. So, he decided they should concentrate on getting the official part over with first and say nothing, but he squeezed her hand gently.

A couple of service sheets were quietly passed across to the betrothed couple by the efficient and forward-thinking best man, then the minister welcomed the congregation.

"It is very pleasing to find a couple who want to have a church wedding these days," he began. "I have, of course, met them twice before, and of all the couples I have had the pleasant duty of marrying over the years, I cannot recall such a loving couple who are so clearly meant for each other."

A few people clapped, acknowledging the minister's kind remarks.

He then went through the service, which proceeded without a hitch. Then he asked Emily, "Will you take this man to be your wedded husband, to live together in Holy Matrimony, will you obey, serve, love, and honour him, in sickness and in health, forsaking all others, so long as you shall live?"

There was then a distinct pause — so much so that Fiona was worried for a moment that Emily was going to say no.

Later, the reason would be explained, but after what seemed like hours, she finally replied "I will," almost shouting the words so no-one was in doubt.

Of course, once they had exchanged rings and had been declared husband and wife, Emily was all smiles. And after a closing hymn, they walked back down the aisle to leave the church, giving hugs and some kisses to close friends. At first, James was very patient, but as she paused yet again to kiss another young man, he said, "Excuse me, my wicked witch, do I get a kiss?"

Emily turned and, feeling a little guilty, said, "Oh, my wee laddie, of course." And she gave him a long loving kiss, which sparked loud cheers and clapping from the congregation.

Releasing himself from the embrace, James announced, "Okay everybody, we will see 28 of you at the Inverbroch Arms for breakfast. And the rest of you should know by now that you are all invited to a ceilidh at about 4pm, in the Inverbroch Community Hall."

Then he took Emily's hand and firmly escorted her into the waiting Rolls Royce for the journey back to Inverbroch. They arrived back just before 12:30pm, and as they went inside a glass of red or white wine, or soft drink was offered.

Of course, there was a lot of chatting and hugs for friends and relatives who had not seen each other for some time.

It is the tradition at Scottish weddings to have the speeches first, with wine waiters ready to fill glasses for the various toasts.

At 1pm, Robert Macdonald rose and welcomed everybody. This was the signal for those who had not yet found their seat to do so quickly, and he waited until the hubbub died down before he began.

"It is a joyous day for a father when their daughter finally leaves the nest. Not, I might add, because she has caused such a commotion that I am looking for some peace and quiet. On the contrary, Emily has always been a thoughtful, helpful child. Furthermore, unlike some parents who may despair about what their child wants to do to earn a living, our Emily has since the age of ten had one aim — to be a ceramicist; she wanted to be a potter. And indeed she is now just that, having won the blue ribbon for the quality of her work at her course in Edinburgh. So, I am rightly very proud of my daughter.

"Of course, the real question is, did she choose the right man to be her husband? Well, I think she has. James is a kind, gentle, loving soul who fell in love with Emily overnight at the ceilidh in August last year. In fact, he was so dazzled by Emily that he could not be sure he was not dreaming. That evening, when he kissed her goodnight, he asked her to leave a glass slipper behind so he could be sure he could find her the next day."

Robert paused to allow a titter of laughter.

"As it happened, the next day we had been invited to the Mackays for tea, so James had the opportunity to check that the shoe he had been given by Emily the night before actually fitted and ensured the dream was continuing. James showed his mettle later when we asked him at tea how they were getting on. He said, and I quote, 'I think I have tamed the wicked witch from the north.'"

At this remark, Robert waited for laughter to die down then he went on. "Some of you will remember that Thomas the Tank Engine had an engine friend named James, but what you may not recall is there was another engine called Emily. So, I checked what they got up to, and three stories stood out.

"The first was called, *James Gives Emily a Scare* — so that rather shows James is no pushover."

More laughter followed.

"The second was called *James in Love,* and the third was called, *James and Emily Have a Goodnight Cuddle.*"

There was much laughter at this last remark.

Then Robert, raising his glass, announced, "I think I have said enough, so a toast to the bride and groom, Emily and James." And he gave way to his new son-in-law.

While James was much more confident these days, he was not used to giving speeches, so he had prepared a few notes which he took from his pocket.

"First of all," he began, "I want to thank you all for coming, and over the last few years for being so friendly and kind to me."

For a moment tears came into his eyes, so he bit his lip and composed himself before continuing.

"Now, it is important to note this meal is called a Wedding Breakfast. When I was younger, and indeed before I had a girlfriend, my father gave me what I thought at the time was a strange bit of advice. He said, 'Don't rush to go out with someone you meet late at night after perhaps drinking too much. But go out with the person you would like to have breakfast with.' Well, I seem to have got that right."

There was plenty of laughter and clapping, so James paused for a moment.

"I hope to have many more breakfasts sitting next to my very beautiful, but very wicked young girl called Emily, who had me on tenterhooks at the church as she waited for what seemed like an eternity before finally saying 'I will'. She has since advised me that she will explain the delay shortly.

"Now, one of my tasks is to thank the bridesmaids, Fiona and Yvonne, for looking after Emily and making sure she was there to say 'I will'... even if there was a long pause."

There was a titter of laughter, so James took the opportunity to have a quick gulp of wine to steady himself before continuing.

"I owe thanks to everybody here, but especially to my and Emily's parents for looking after me and — unbeknown to me — apparently hoping we two would get together. I had thought I was under the spell of the wicked witch, but it seems there was a degree of an arranged marriage. But, if that is true, I have no objection."

At this point he nodded in the direction of the parents to acknowledge he was happy with the situation.

"Of course, I also have to thank my best man for quietly ensuring everything ran smoothly, although of course I have not read what he may say about me. You may also be aware that since the night of the ceilidh, Emily has constantly been saying she will look after me. But I feel quite guilty sometimes, feeling the shoes should be on the other feet... not glass slippers, though."

There was a lot of laughter at this remark before James brought his short speech to a close. Raising his glass, he said, "A toast to you all, but especially to Fiona and Yvonne."

Allan did not immediately rise to give his best man speech, especially as a few were already needing to take a comfort break. Instead, he asked the waiters to ensure everybody's glass was fully charged, then waited for five minutes before getting to his feet.

As everyone always expects a good speech from the best man at any wedding, there was a degree of hushed anticipation.

Allan began formally, "Ladies and gentlemen," but then he quickly made a joke by continuing, "honoured guests, and fairy godmother and wicked witch. I come to praise James, not to be unkind to him, for he is an honourable man. In fact, he has always been a kind and gentle fellow, who up until a year ago would not say boo to a goose. "

There was some laughter and clapping at these remarks, but he continued.

"However, a year is a long time when you are engaged, and it seems he has learnt how to deflect the spells of his betrothed — so much so, according to his father-in-law, that it seems James actually scared the wicked Emily."

Allan paused for laughter.

"When we were younger, and bear in mind I am nearly two years older, it was me who often led him astray. But he was not backward in coming forward and would swing from the branches of our neighbour's apple tree like a trained chimpanzee, scrounging all the best apples without his feet touching the ground on the neighbour's side of the fence.

"While my strengths are in maths and economics, James was always looking for the next scene to sketch. And there were many times our parents thought we were very quiet and had gone to bed early, when in practice we were out looking for suitable views across the loch.

"On one occasion he wanted to sketch the sunset across Tongue Bay. I remember on that evening he was adamant that we needed to get further north so he could get Castle Varrich in the picture. The problem was not doing the sketch, or taking into account the dying light, it was finding we had been locked out when we got back to the house at about 10:30pm. And we were forced to knock on the door to be let in, pretending we had only slipped out for a breath of fresh air. I can see my parents smiling, as they now realise, they were duped that night.

"Now, you may think Emily is the wicked one here, but I think now is the time we two county men should come clean and resolve the mystery of the 'phantom bicycle thief of Tongue Bay', which was the title of the story printed in the local rag six or seven years ago.

"I had a bicycle, but when James came to stay, often for several days in the summer holidays, the question was where to get another bicycle for him to use? We had a police station in Tongue, but it was only manned some of the time and rarely on Saturdays. The policemen had bicycles parked behind the police station, but they were rarely used because they also had a police car. The problem was two-fold: they were normal adult-size bikes, and also had a number lock on them."

He paused to look around the room. "Perhaps I should not be telling you this, but if you are clever, you can determine the number by pulling on the chain holding the padlock with one hand, then very slowly turn each numbered segment until it goes slightly loose. You do this to each of the number rings and, hey presto, you now know the number. James has long, dextrous, sensitive fingers and was a dab hand at finding the correct number in only a few minutes. So, looking around to ensure nobody was about, we were round the back of the police station and — often in only six or seven minutes — both up the road on a bicycle.

"James, of course, has always been quite tall so he did not find it difficult to use his purloined velocipede. We would cycle up to Weavers Café about 1½ miles uphill and have a fizzy drink and an ice cream. The journey back was fun as it was all downhill. What we did not appreciate, while we were enjoying our trip out, was that the local Police Inspector had come to do an inventory, and he recorded one lady's bicycle.

"The next day, when the Inspector queried who rode the lady's bicycle, the local policeman said, 'We do not have a lady, and anyway I use the gent's bike!' Of course, the Inspector said no gent's bicycle was there during his visit!

"We were careful to leave the bicycle where we'd found it, duly locked with the number lock, which we did after the Inspector had left. Scratching his head, the local Sergeant could not quite understand why the Inspector had not seen the gent's bike! We did this on several occasions, so much so that the local rag carried a story about a phantom bicycle thief.

"So, if you think Emily is wicked, you can see they are very well suited, being as wicked as each other."

There was much laughter at this story unfolded and especially at this last comment.

Allan went on, "Of course, I understand Emily will often say, 'No good turn goes unpunished, and equally no bad turn goes unrewarded.' On one occasion, we found there was a puncture in the bike's front wheel and we quietly mended it — so you see, we were not totally wicked. However, on another occasion, we were nearly caught out. We arrived at the café to find neighbours of ours who had walked up to Weavers, and they were slightly flummoxed when they realised that they would have to carry all their new purchases back the 1½ miles. So, we volunteered to take their shopping back on our bikes and deliver it to their backdoor. As we were about to leave, they commented, 'That looks just like the bicycle the police sergeant rides!' James quickly comes up with this amazing story about always having his bike stolen so deliberately painting it to look like a police bike to put off would-be thieves. 'Oh,' they said, 'that's clever.' And they fell for his story hook, line, and sinker."

A few clapped at this story, acknowledging James's clever deception.

"Now, Emily tells me James is sure this is all a dream. She also tells me — from her almost telepathic knowledge — that other people here today are thinking they must also be dreaming. So, I finish my epistle with a rather unusual toast: to ensure the dream continues, please raise your glasses.

"The dream."

For a moment there were puzzled faces, then realising what Allan meant, they entered into the spirit of the occasion and did as they were bid.

Allan then said, "I can see many of you are getting quite peckish, so let the feasting begin."

This was the signal the waiters had been waiting for. While the speeches were being made, the waiters had quietly been around to determine if people wanted the Laphroaig-cured salmon or the lobster bisque. Placing a soup spoon down where appropriate, this meant the starters could be served quickly.

The next course surprised many people who had eaten at the hotel before, because the first choice was the most expensive dish on the menu — Saddle of Highland Venison with all the trimmings. The alternative, to cater for the very few vegetarians, was Butternut Squash Risotto, although it was served with pumpkin seeds and pine nuts, so the waiters were primed to ask should anybody choose this option that they did not have a nut allergy. Most of the toasts had been taken with champagne like white wine. This meant as the venison was served, red wine was offered.

There was, of course, quite a hubbub with 30 people all chatting. Aileen was sitting at a table for four, along with Calum and Charlotte Gordon and Jane McCready.

Aileen could not but notice the handsome Bestman. She whispered, "Does anybody know the name of the best man?"

Charlotte had been introduced to him, as he had dutifully taken the trouble to welcome them and escort them to their table, so she advised Aileen he was James's cousin Allan Mackay.

Aileen's eyes widened. "Another county man?" she replied. "Does anybody know if he has a girlfriend, as I don't see a likely partner sitting near him?"

Charlotte, of course, could see that young Aileen was already keen to meet him. So, smiling, she said, "It looks like I might have to be a fairy godmother again."

Aileen was slightly embarrassed, realising those at the table now knew her interest in him was more than platonic, so she stopped talking and hoped someone would change the subject.

But Jane McCready actually encouraged her. "He looks like a man in need of the gentle touch of a young girl like you. Don't you worry, my dear, I am sure he will be more than happy to be your partner at the ceilidh later."

What Aileen didn't notice was that Charlotte quickly scribbled a message and asked one of the waiters to carefully hand it to Emily.

In due course, plates from the main course were collected up, and orders for the dessert were obtained and quickly satisfied. The choices were Bramble and Vanilla Cheesecake, various flavours of ice cream, or Scottish Cheese Platter. Then the coffee was served.

By that time, Emily had not only decided what to say but had given secret instructions for a couple of surprises to take place when she gave a signal to one of the young waiters, as if she was casting a spell.

She rose from her seat, and in order to attract everyone's attention tinkled a spoon against a couple of glasses. It was not necessarily expected that the bride would speak, but at the same time many thought they were not going to get away without a few words from the former Head Girl.

She began by announcing in a quiet but forceful voice, "Today is a wonderful day, as today at last I have my James finally by my side as my wonderful, artistic, and kind husband. Only a few of you will know I have looked forward to this day for over five years. I can see some of you doing the maths, as I am only 22 and James is still only 20. Thus, the astute among you will be saying, 'I am not sure it would be legal that long ago.' You would, of course, be right, as my James was a quiet, shy 15-year-old. However, some of you will also know I can be very patient and determined.

"Now this leads me on to why a few hours ago there was this earth-shattering pause. I could almost feel those around me at church, wondering if I was ever going to say 'I will'.

"Let me ask you a question. How many times does a young girl have to say she wishes to marry a very handsome young county man? The answer is four times. Yes, I know I only said

'Yes' or 'I will' once in church, but since the night of the ceilidh it has been four times. I don't think my beautiful husband will mind if I say that he fell in love with me on the night of the ceilidh. However, he could not be sure he was not dreaming, so having escorted me home, he asked me to leave one of my glass slippers behind so he could find me the next day."

Emily paused for a titter of laughter.

"At the time I was temporarily fresh out of glass slippers, so I tossed him one of the black shoes I had been wearing. The next day, when Katherine had kindly asked us Macdonalds to tea, James insists on checking that my foot fitted the shoe he had kept. Of course, it did exactly. So, James said, 'I think that means you have to marry me.' Well, how could a young girl say no to this handsome man?

"A little later, James wanted to show me something up the Great Glen Way, so we walked up the very steep hill and along to a short track that leads off the long-distance trail and you arrive at a very large stone seat, now called St Columba's Seat as St Columba's saint's day is my birthday, the 9th of June. As I sat down, I shouted to him, 'We're in the picture, we are sitting in the picture! I realise now who the person in the picture is with an orange hat, it is your father.' Well, I have to say, James was temporally overcome as this was where he had last sat for any time with his father. He had painted the picture for the school competition and won the prize."

"Now to explain. I regularly went into the art class after school and took, with the art teacher's blessing, any pictures that I thought worth keeping, nearly all of which were by my artistic husband. This was on the basis that they would be thrown away after a couple of days, if not claimed by the student. It just happened that as it was the end of term when James won the competition, and the art teacher was busy with end of term reports, I took the prize picture, and I always felt there was

151

something a little magical about it. James did not know I had the picture, so once my poor laddie had composed himself, he asked how I knew about the picture. 'Because,' I said, 'it is hanging on my bedroom wall.' Trying to comfort him, I said it was okay if he wanted to have it back. At which point, James said, 'It's okay you can keep it, as long as you marry me.' Of course, I said I would but pointed out I had already agreed to marry him less than two hours before."

Emily paused to let the story sink in, with many smiling or laughing, but then continued.

"Now the third time was where we were lucky enough to come across the Gordons. It was in this very building, sitting at a table over there, when James asked me to marry him for the third time, and he gave me my beautiful engagement ring."

"Now, if I hold up my finger, you will see it is almost identical to the ring Charlotte Gordon is wearing."

Charlotte held up her finger to show everybody how similar the rings were.

"Can I ask you all to raise your glasses and congratulate Calum and Charlotte," Emily continued, "as today is actually their sixty-first wedding anniversary."

Glasses were duly raised and Emily started clapping and everybody joined in.

After a brief pause, she began speaking again. "We actually got engaged on the 2nd of September, but last year the 31st of August was a Thursday, so the Gordons had their celebrations for their sixtieth on the following Saturday. Charlotte was touched by us celebrating our betrothal and kindly sent a couple of glasses of bubbly over to us so we could toast both our engagement and their diamond anniversary. We went over to them, at a large table set out for their family, to thank them for their kind thought, and it was then we saw that our rings matched. It was like she was a fairy godmother, saying we could look forward to at least 60 happy years, or 61 now.

"I can see many of you wondering if I am going to say why a few hours ago, when the Reverend Benjamine Becula asked if I would take my wonderful James to be my wedded husband, there was this long delay. It was simply a case of my thinking through all the previous occasions I had agreed, and I felt like saying; How many times do I need to say yes?"

Emily allowed a brief moment of laughter.

"So you see, the delay was because I temporarily went through the previous three occasions in my head, then in my almost dream-like state realised I had kept all you lot waiting. I know Fiona was having kittens, so I thought I had better make sure everybody was in no doubt, and I said loudly, 'I will.'

"Now you all know the reason for the delay, and that brings me to a few announcements that I need to make. Firstly, you are all welcome to come over to the community hall for a ceilidh, where you may recognise the flowers decorating the hall. Unusually, we will start with a waltz so that our sixty-firsters can join in, because Charlotte said when we invited them that they are no longer up to dancing the Dashing White Sergeant!"

There was a brief moment of laughter at this remark.

"However, before we go over there, I need to wave my wand and sprinkle a little fairy dust about. You will appreciate we have two county men here today. There is, of course, my husband, but also Allan, the best man, is also a Mackay. And I can announce he has just passed his exams and is now a qualified accountant."

Emily then led a moment of clapping to congratulate him. "There is a certain young lady who will be most intrigued by this touch of serendipity, as she too is studying accountancy and will be hoping to have a dance with him."

With that, Emily lifted her hand as a signal, and there was a loud pop behind Aileen who gave out a shriek of surprise as a shower of gold petals fell around her.

"Your wish is granted," Emily said, much to the amusement of everyone near the table.

Aileen, however, thought to herself; *There is a God, there is a God*.

However, while everybody's gaze was focused on the slightly embarrassed Aileen, there came another loud pop behind Fiona. At first, she thought it must be a mistake, before realising that Matthew had slipped off his chair and was now kneeling beside her.

"Will you marry me?" he asked.

Fiona gave a shriek of surprise and said, "Of course, my wee laddie." Then quietly, added just to Matthew, "About time, too," giving him a kiss while he was still kneeling rather awkwardly on the floor.

After a chorus of clapping and shouts of congratulations, Emily brought her long epistle to a close. "I have temporarily run out of fairy dust, so we will see you all over at the hall shortly."

As Emily finished, she went over to congratulate Fiona and Matthew on their engagement, giving her best friend a hug and Matthew a kiss on the cheek.

There was no immediate rush to go across the road to the ceilidh, but after about 20 minutes, Emily said to James, "Perhaps we should lead the way?" And as soon as it was clear that the bride and groom were off to dance, most people followed.

At the hall, James asked the band to play a slow waltz to allow everybody to enjoy the first dance with their chosen partner. Of course, Aileen rushed up to Allan, who seemed delighted to be so clearly favoured by the Irish lassie. Nearly everybody there got up to dance with somebody. The Gordons were pleased to be able to join in, as was Jane McCready who partnered with Robert Macdonald, as Margaret was busy organising the food.

Sarah Mackay, Allan's mother, also felt she should help with the food, and this left Allan's father, Roger, free to dance with his sister-in-law, Katherine.

Quite a few of the men swapped partners, first with James and then whoever had stolen the beaming bride, just to say they got a dance with the bonnie wee lass.

After this first introductory dance, the ceilidh really kicked off with the Gay Gordons, quickly followed by the Dashing White Sergeant.

A year ago, James would have very tentatively asked a girl to dance with him, but now he only had to smile in their direction, and they instantly took his hand. He no longer felt he might lose his wonderful lassie and could choose any girl to be his partner. In like fashion, Emily would be dragging any laddie that melted as she smiled at them out onto the floor to dance.

After five dances, concluding with the Virginia Reel, most were pleased to take a seat and enjoy some of the fare offered by the Inverbroch baking ladies — a group who offered their services to provide tasty dishes for similar events.

At 8pm, a taxi arrived to take the Gordons home. Emily and James made a point of thanking them for coming, as they truly felt blessed by their presence.

There were only a couple of dances after the food was served, and of course James and Emily joined hands for the last of the evening. Then at 8:30pm, a taxi arrived for the newlyweds and they bade farewell to everybody, with kisses for their parents.

"Where are we going?" asked Emily.

"Oh, don't worry, the driver knows the way," said James. "If we are lucky, we should have the view of the sunset over the Beauly Firth at dinner — not today, but tomorrow, as I have booked for three nights. Sorry, it's not longer, my love, but my funds are a bit stretched at the moment. However, by the summer next year we should be able to take at least a week at a place of your choice. However, it is a four-star establishment, and we have one of their best rooms."

"But where are we actually going?" Emily repeated.

"I can see you did not concentrate on your geography at school," laughed James. "It's where the dream continues, my beautiful wife." And gave her a hug and a long loving kiss.

*The End, or is it?*

# Epilogue

I can hear many of you shouting that the story can't end there! But many dreams end quite suddenly. Was it a dream, or did it all really happen?

Let me ask some questions. Have you identified the name of the town in the Great Glen? Have you ever been to the Orange Berries café? Is there a place called Cut Lake? And is there a wee chalet there called *Shed and Breakfast*?

Well, let me put you out of your misery and read these entries I discovered in Katherine's diary.

*Friday, 27th May, 2027*

Wonderful day. Emily had her twins – Lucy, 4lbs 4oz, and Gordon, 4lbs 1oz, both doing well. Emily very relieved, last few weeks she has been quite anxious, but all smiles now. James also delighted. They were delivered a few weeks early by C-section.

*Tuesday, 20th August, 2030*

Twin's first day at school, looking very grown-up and smart in school uniform, Gordon holding tightly onto big sister Lucy as they go in. However, Emily tells me they were all smiles when she collected them. Gordon holding his first piece of artwork at school, which already shows he will be an artist as good as his father.

*Tuesday, 17th December, 2030*

The twins starting to show their individuality. Lucy loved helping me put up some Christmas decorations and has already shown a certain artistic bent. I left her briefly in the kitchen, while I took James and Emily their morning coffee and biscuits and some for wee Gordon. I found Gordon sitting beside his father in front of the little easel James had made for him. He was very carefully trying to imitate his father, and the result was a recognisable picture, already showing signs that he appreciates perspective and light and shade. I returned to the kitchen to find Lucy dancing round to the music on Classic FM, being Eliza's Aria with a big smile on her face. As we stopped for a drink and biscuit, she asked, 'What's a dream?' Oh, I said, that's when you're asleep and loverly things happen, although you may need a touch of serendipity. 'What's serenzipitty?' she asked, 'And do dreams come true?' Definitely, I replied. You ask your father; he has been dreaming for more than seven years!

# About the Author

**Peter Gatenby** is not yet known as an imaginative and inventive author, but more as the man who has walked everywhere. He will tell you he may be the only person living or dead who in 2012/13 walked from his front door to the furthest points — East, West, South, and North — of the British mainland, known as the Extremities. Five years later, he went to the Sharp Corners, as he calls them — the furthest Southwest, Southeast, Northeast, and Northwest. The story of these epic treks will not appear in print form for some years but will be covered under the title *The Three Blue Plaques*. These plaques record the foregoing achievement and currently adorn the cottage wall where he lives. In the meantime, you can still glean a lot from the websites set up to monitor these walks: www.theextremities.co.uk and www.thesharpcorners.co.uk

The first short story to be published by the author, at the beginning of 2023, was *Married by Lunchtime* — a light-hearted romance with a few unusual twists and turns. The next volume, *La Nuit a Therouanne,* is another book of fiction, about the struggle to bring to justice a rapist and murderer. Both these stories are fictional but cleverly keep the reader wondering until the last few pages how the issues raised will be resolved.

Another book yet to be published is based on real family history, starting in 1910, following the writer's maiden great-aunts who went to Singapore in 1925. There is no clever scheme to make it have a satisfying resolution, perhaps more a *Quantum of Solace,* the full story has been written although small, apparently insignificant pieces of information keep turning up. Thus, it might be considered more of a documentary about one family living through the early and middle parts of the 20th century; often being a living detective story.

The time period is so long, and it fills so many pages, that it is now being structured as six episodes under the collective banner of *The Farrells of Banchory House.* This house — the family home — stood in Old Dover Road, Blackheath, but was severely damaged by a V2 in WWII and later demolished to make way for the A102 underpass. The race is now on to try and find a picture of the house before the book goes to press.

A new short story — the volume you have just purchased — was written to try and redress the balance against all the terrible stories you read in the press almost every day. So, the author hopes *St Columba's Seat and a Touch of Serendipity* will leave readers with a smile on their face.

Peter's working life of 43+ years was in Financial Services, and at the time of his retirement in 2006 he was a Fellow of the Chartered Insurance Institute and an Associate of the Compliance Institute, as well as an Associate of the Personal Finance Society.

Nowadays, he is a member of two ramblers groups and is a Churchwarden. (He has previously been Churchwarden on three occasions, totalling 10 years' service). He was also the Chairman of The Mill Stream Villages Association (see www.TMSVA.co.uk) although the responsibility for the signs has now moved to the local Parish Council of Wookey.

When not writing or walking he is the proud father of four children and eight grandchildren. A full house, when adding in husbands, wives, boyfriends, and girlfriends, currently stands at 22, although eldest grandson George is in Canada for another year with his fiancée Nora.

The skills being developed by both his children and grandchildren ensure that the above volumes can be marketed and even, in due course, turned into short films!

In an attempt to bring all the above together, you can go to www.petergatenby.co.uk — although this is very much a work in progress.

www.ingramcontent.com/pod-product-compliance
Lightning Source LLC
Chambersburg PA
CBHW051827040426
42447CB00006B/402